REAL CITY

Berlin

REAL CITY

Berlin

www.realcity.dk.com

LONDON, NEW YORK,
MELBOURNE, MUNICH AND DELHI
www.dk.com

Produced by
Blue Island Publishing

Contributors
Natalie Gravenor, Constance Hanna, Jürgen Scheunemann

Photographers
Britta Jaschinski, Hans Kwiotek

Reproduced in Singapore by Colourscan
Printed and bound in Singapore by Tien Wah Press

First published in Great Britain in 2007
by Dorling Kindersley Limited
80 Strand, London WC2R 0RL

A CIP catalogue record is available from the British Library.

ISBN: 978-1-40531-795-5

The information in this Real City guide is checked annually.

This guide is supported by a dedicated website which provides the very latest information for visitors
to Berlin; please see page 7 for the web address and password. Some information, however,
is liable to change, and the publishers cannot accept responsibility for any consequences arising
from the use of this book, nor for any material on third party websites, and cannot guarantee that
any website address in this book will be a suitable source of travel information.
We value the views and suggestions of our readers very highly. Please write to:
Publisher, DK Eyewitness Travel Guides,
Dorling Kindersley, 80 Strand, London WC2R 0RL, Great Britain.

Contents

The Guide

Real City Berlin

Stay ahead of the crowd with **Real City Berlin**, and find the best places to eat, shop, drink and chill out at a glance.

The guide is divided into four main sections:

Introducing Berlin – essential background information on the city, including an overview by one of the authors, the top tourist attractions, festivals and seasonal events, and useful travel and practical information.

Listings – eight themed chapters packed with incisive reviews of the best the city has to offer, in every price band and chosen by local experts.

Street Finder – map references in the listings lead you to this section, where you can plan your route and find your way around.

Indexes – the By Area and By Type indexes offer shortcuts to what you are looking for, whether it is a bar in Charlottenburg or a Turkish restaurant.

The Website

www.realcity.dk.com

By purchasing this book you have been granted free access to up-to-the-minute online content about Berlin for at least 12 months. Click onto **www.realcity.dk.com** for updates, and sign up for a free weekly email with the latest information on what to see and do in Berlin.

On the website you can:

- **Find the latest news** about Berlin, including exhibitions, restaurant openings and music events

- Check what other readers have to say and **add your own comments** and reviews

- **Plan your visit** with a customizable calendar

- See at a glance **what's in and what's not**

- Look up listings by name, by type and by area, and check the **latest reviews**

- **Link directly** to all the websites in the book, and many more

How to register

> Click on the Berlin icon on the home page of the website to register or log in.

> Enter the city code given on this page, and follow the instructions given.

> The city code will be valid for a minimum of 12 months from the date you purchased this guide.

city code: **berlin82561**

introducing berlin

Declared capital of the reunified Germany in 1991 after decades of turmoil, Berlin is now being reinvented. The city is a crucible for daring architects, designers, artists and dramatists, along with creative hoteliers and restaurateurs. This guide leads you to Berlin's latest and best, beginning with the top attractions, and events and celebrations throughout the year.

INTRODUCING BERLIN

Berlin is back and better than ever, and the once divided city where East meets West is again among the world's top creative and fashionable destinations. Berlin is still changing at a staggering pace: Berliners have seen it all and are easily bored, so the stakes are increasing year by year. Myriad events come and go in a constant flow, and as the city firmly establishes itself as one of the international cultural hotspots, there couldn't be a better time to visit.

Jürgen Scheunemann

The Ever-Changing City

"Berlin will never be, but always remain in the making." This famous Berlin saying was coined at the dawn of the 20th century and it applies equally at the dawn of the 21st. The speed of change, dramatically accelerated after the fall of the Berlin Wall in 1989, may have slowed down a little, but the flurry of new buildings, changed street names and grand projects can still be felt. The city seems to reinvent itself every other year or so. It has always been that way, primarily because of its location, at the crossroads between Eastern and Western Europe. It attracts visitors from both cultural spheres, many of whom come to stay. Indeed the influx of the creative and the curious continues to nurture Berlin's appetite for new trends, and districts such as the Scheunenviertel in Mitte, parts of Kreuzberg, the new, hot district of Friedrichshain, and the glitzy façades along Kurfürstendamm and around Potsdamer Platz symbolize the vibrant diversity of a rejuvenated city. At the same time, Berlin is proud of its down-to-earth, no-nonsense attitude, which is expressed in the dry, often aggressive humour and slang we Berliners use, particularly regarding our own city.

Berlin's Cultural Buzz

Thanks to its past as Imperial German capital, Berlin has amassed some of the world's finest collections of antique art from the Middle East, as well as medieval paintings, cultural treasures from the 18th and 19th centuries, and some of the best modern art too. Grand Baroque and Rococo palaces, such as Sanssouci and the Charlottenburg Palace, are matched by top contemporary international architecture, just as the time-honoured art collections are challenged by today's cutting-edge creations in art, theatre, film, dance, performance, fashion, music and literature. Berlin is a hotbed for creative minds who are inspired by the city's openness and edgy flair – the famous "Berliner Luft" (or "anything goes" attitude). Berliners love art and make a receptive audience. It's a way of life and a great social equalizer in a city that is poor in Western terms, but where art is nevertheless heavily state-subsidized.

a city primer

A night at the Philharmonic, a Sunday at the Neue Nationalgalerie or an evening opening at a contemporary art gallery all tend to bring out the most diverse, but equally knowledgeable, audiences.

Ich bin ein Berliner

Berlin used to be one of Europe's most cosmopolitan cities, thanks in part to the presence of Allied powers in West Berlin during the Cold War. Those days are over, but with foreign embassies and many international organizations now based in the city, Berlin is fast regaining its cosmopolitan character. A total of 460,000 foreigners representing 182 nations live here (roughly 18 per cent of the city's population), and each can now claim "Ich bin ein Berliner". Turkey provides the biggest group, and Turkish culture and food has permeated daily life, especially in neighbourhoods like Neukölln and Kreuzberg. The presence of all these nations substantially adds to the quality of life, most readily seen in the ethnic restaurants and *Imbisse* (small eatery stands found everywhere in the city).

Clubbers' Paradise

Berlin is one big, hot volcano of party fun. Alongside the plethora of bars, the city has a diverse selection of clubs where any imaginable nightlife excess can be experienced. Since Christopher Isherwood described Berlin's ecstatic nightlife in his *Berlin Diaries* (later made into the musical and film *Cabaret*), the city has enjoyed a reputation for its lascivious pleasures. Today, this party continues in a more modern and hip way – thanks to the young from all over Europe who flock here. There is no official closing hour in Berlin, and the nightlife starts late and continues till the sun comes up. Berlin is a rough and raw city, but while other capitals are steeped in tradition, Berlin is always a step ahead, creating new, funky trends.

✅ The Good Value Mark

Cities can be expensive, but if you know where to go you can always discover excellent-value places. We've picked out the best of these in the Restaurants, Shopping and Hotels chapters and indicated them with the pink Good Value mark.

INTRODUCING BERLIN

The German capital offers world-class museums, churches and architecture, as well as charming parks and bustling neighbourhoods full of cultural life and new dynamism. However, despite the rapidity of change in the landscape of Berlin, there remain certain enduring landmarks that are instantly recognizable – places that every visitor should see at least once. These are the attractions with perennial appeal, the city's most unmissable sights.

Kulturforum
9 A1

030 20 90 55 55 • Ⓢ Ⓤ Potsdamer Platz
≫ www.smb.spk-berlin.de

A complex of museums, galleries and concert halls – including the Gemäldegalerie *(see p78)*, Neue Nationalgalerie *(see p77)*, Staatsbibliothek *(see p75)* and Philharmonie *(see p91)* – the Kulturforum was first established in the 1950s.

Museumsinsel
6 E2

Bodestrasse 1–3 • 030 20 90 55 55 • Ⓢ Hackescher Markt
≫ www.museumsinsel-berlin.de Open 10am–6pm Tue–Sun (to 10pm Thu)

The Museum Island is a cluster of five museums comprising the Alte Nationalgalerie *(see p71)*, the Altes Museum (Greco-Roman and Egyptian collection), the Bodemuseum (coin collection and Byzantine art), the Neues Museum and the Pergamonmuseum *(see p70)*.

Jüdisches Museum
9 D2

Lindenstrasse 9–14 • 030 25 99 33 00 • Ⓤ Hallesches Tor
≫ www.jmberlin.de Open 10am–8pm daily (to 10pm Mon)

Daniel Libeskind's zig-zagging, zinc-clad construction houses an amazing collection that documents two millennia of Jewish culture in Germany. The museum is both a celebration of Jewish-German achievements, artistically and commercially, and a reminder of the hardships and terror Jews suffered here *(see p82)*.

For the very latest on Berlin go to ≫ www.realcity.dk.com

top attractions

Unter den Linden

5 C3

🅂 Unter den Linden

This grand boulevard is one of Berlin's most prestigious avenues, lined with historic buildings, museums and sights, beginning at the western end with the Brandenburger Tor. In the 1920s, the avenue was the bustling downtown heart of Berlin; today it is an inviting place to stroll and to relax in street-side cafés *(see p124).*

Brandenburger Tor

5 C3

Pariser Platz • 🅂 Unter den Linden

This iconic gate was built in 1791. It is the only remaining city gate and the quintessential symbol of Berlin. Napoleon celebrated his victory over Prussia here in 1806, the Nazis began their infamous torch march at the gate in 1933, and hundreds of thousands cheered German reunification here in 1989 *(see p124).*

Reichstag

5 A3

Platz der Republik 1 • 030 22 73 21 52 • 🅂 Unter den Linden
➤➤ www.bundestag.de Open 8am to midnight daily

The Reichstag was built for the parliament of the newly unified German Empire in 1894 by Paul Wallot. Destroyed in World War II, the Reichstag was later reconstructed and finally restored to glory in 1999, complete with a new glass dome by British architect Sir Norman Foster. The Reichstag is now home to the German federal parliament.

➤➤ *Unter den Linden was laid out as a route between the city palace and royal hunting grounds in the Tiergarten*

INTRODUCING BERLIN

Schloss Charlottenburg `1 B4`

Spandauer Damm 22–4 • 030 32 09 14 40 • Ⓤ Richard-Wagner-Platz
≫ www.spsg.de Open 9am–5pm Tue–Sun

The Charlottenburg Palace, built as a royal summer residence in the late 17th and 18th centuries by Prussia's finest architects, is one of Europe's most beautiful Baroque palaces. The grand gardens are a popular green retreat for picnicking Berliners *(see p80).* **Adm**

Checkpoint Charlie `9 D1`

Friedrichstrasse 43–5 • 030 25 37 25 0 • Ⓤ Kochstrasse
≫ www.mauermuseum.de Open 9am–10pm daily

Checkpoint Charlie is a potent symbol of the Cold War and of a city – and indeed continent – divided. Next to a replica control booth stands the Haus am Checkpoint Charlie, a museum that tells the fascinating story of the Berlin Wall and the ingenious attempts to cross it. **Adm**

Tiergarten `2 G5`

Strasse des 17 Juni • Ⓢ Tiergarten

The Tiergarten is 495 acres (200 ha) of green parks, woodlands, lakes, a river and historic monuments in the heart of Berlin. Originally royal hunting grounds, the Tiergarten was transformed into a public park by architect Peter Joseph Lenné in the 1830s. At its centre, the Siegessäule, one of Berlin's most famous landmarks, celebrates German victories in the late 19th century *(see p134).*

top attractions

Kaiser-Wilhelm-Gedächtnis-Kirche `8 F2`
Breitscheidplatz • 030 21 85 02 3 • Ⓢ Ⓤ Zoologischer Garten
≫ www.gedaechtniskirche.com Open 9am–7pm daily

The Kaiser Wilhelm Memorial Church, built in 1895 in honour of the late Emperor Wilhelm I and all but destroyed in World War II, now stands as a sobering reminder of the terror of war. The massive bell tower, nicknamed "hollow tooth", is joined to a 1960s hall *(see p79)*. **Adm**

Zoologischer Garten `8 F1`
Hardenbergplatz 8 • 030 25 40 10 • Ⓢ Ⓤ Zoologischer Garten
≫ www.zoo-berlin.de Open Mar–Oct: 9am–6:30pm daily;
Nov–Feb: 9am–5pm daily

Highlights of Berlin's zoo include the gorillas and chimps, the pandas and the adjoining aquarium, which offers a walk on a hanging bridge through an artificial rain forest – with alligators dozing below. **Adm**

Potsdamer Platz `5 A5`
Ⓢ Ⓤ Potsdamer Platz
≫ www.potsdamer-platz.net

The Potsdamer Platz, built on a once deserted spot in the shadow of the Berlin Wall, is now the vibrant modern heart of Berlin. Highrises and glitzy architecture by David Chipperfield, Helmut Jahn, Renzo Piano and Hans Kollhoff have created a new city quarter, complete with cinemas, shopping complexes and restaurants *(see p124)*.

≫ *Berlin's zoo houses some 1,500 different kinds of animals – the largest number of any zoo in the world*

INTRODUCING BERLIN

Berlin is at its finest in the spring and summer, when Berliners spend as much time as possible outside. From June to August there are numerous outdoor events, many of which are free. The best of the large organized events are listed below, but you may well stumble on an impromptu neighbourhood festival or a performance in a park. And countless bars and cafés offer the opportunity for alfresco eating and drinking *(see p116)*.

Theatertreffen Berlin

www.berlinerfestspiele.de

This major theatre festival has been running since 1963 and showcases exciting new productions from German-speaking countries at various venues. **May**

Karneval der Kulturen

www.karneval-berlin.de

Kreuzberg celebrates the city's multi-culturalism with a street party, costume parade, music, food and crafts from many countries. **May or Jun**

Lesbisch-schwules Stadtfest Berlin & Berlin Christopher Street Day

Nollendorfplatz & Motzstrasse in Schöneberg (Map 8 H2)
www.regenbogenfonds.de • www.csd-berlin.de
English language info: 030 23 62 86 32

Gay and lesbian Berliners unite to celebrate pride and strength. The festival includes performances, exhibitions and talks, and culminates with a huge, friendly street fair in Schöneberg on the third Sunday in June. **Jun**

Fête de la Musique Berlin

www.fetedelamusique.de • 030 41 71 52 89

In a tradition that originated in France, the night of the summer solstice sees dozens of music venues across Berlin opening their doors for free. **21 Jun**

Deutsch-Französische Volksfest

Zentraler Festplatz, Kurt-Schumacher-Damm (Map 1 B1)
www.berliner-volksfeste.de • 030 21 33 29 0

In the aftermath of World War II, Berliners were exposed to the cultures of the occupying Allied forces, and one positive result was a couple of festivals that continue to this day. The German-French festival has a different theme each year, such as a region or custom of France, and a fairground is always set up. **Mid-Jun–mid-Jul**

Classic Open Air Berlin

Gendarmenmarkt (Map 5 D4) • www.classicopenair.de
Info 030 31 57 54 0 • Tickets 030 31 57 54 13

A variety of opera, light classical and pop music is performed by members of Berlin's symphony orchestras,

spring and summer

framed by the Neo-Classical architecture of the Gendarmenmarkt's historic buildings. **Late Jun–early Jul**

Deutsch-Amerikanische Volksfest
Clayallee and Argentinische Allee in Dahlem
www.deutsch-amerikanisches-volksfest.de • 0163 39 00 93 0

Usually drawing larger crowds than the French festival *(see above)*, the American one has a Wild West theme, with cowboys galore. **Mid-Jul–mid-Aug**

Heimatklänge
Kulturforum (Map 9 B1) & other venues • 0180 51 70 51 7

A showcase for the emerging talent of world music, Heimatklänge is programmed around loose themes, such as "Sinbad's Voyages" or "Wedding Music". **End Jul**

Bewag City & Balisto Skate Nights
Ku'damm (Map 8 F2); Branderburger Tor (Map 5 A3)
www.scc-events.com • www.skate-night-berlin.com

Berliners love all forms of skating, and on Bewag City Night there is a sponsored inline-skating race on Ku'damm that draws up to 50,000 spectators. Balisto Skate Nights take place on Sundays throughout the summer and are mass skate-ins at which young and old alike enter into the fun. **Early Aug**

Tanz im August
www.tanzimaugust.de • 030 24 74 97 58

Top choreographers from around the world join some of Berlin's best for a series of contemporary dance shows, workshops and parties, staged at various venues around the city. **Early Aug–early Sep**

Lange Nacht der Museen
www.lange-nacht-der-museen.de • 030 90 26 99 44 4

More than 100 museums in Berlin and Potsdam stay open long into the night while visitors – over 100,000 each year – ride special shuttle buses from one to the next. It's not a free event, but tickets include the shuttle buses and special programmes. The winter version focuses on the museums in central Berlin.
Last Sat in Aug & last Sat in Jan

INTRODUCING BERLIN

As the days become cooler, Berliners move indoors. Music festivals such as PopKomm, Musikfest and JazzFest cheer up the autumn evenings, and delightful Christmas markets are the highlight of December. The "Berlinale" film festival is a winter fixture, while the increasing popularity of events such as Art Forum Berlin, Lange Nacht der Museen *(see p17)* and Transmediale Germany reinforces Berlin's ascendancy in the world of contemporary art.

Golden League Athletics & Berlin Marathon

Olympiastadion *(see p81)* • www.istaf.de • www.scc-events.com

Since its founding in 1921, ISTAF's Golden League meet has been one of the world's top track-and-field events. Later in the month, both amateurs and professionals gather for the Berlin Marathon. **Sep**

PopKomm Music Festival

www.popkomm.de • www.messe-berlin.com

Berlin snatched PopKomm from Cologne in 2004. It's a trade fair for the German record industry, but anyone can attend the gigs by up-and-coming acts. Venues include the Messe Berlin halls west of Halensee (Map 7 A2) and the Kulturbrauerei *(see p131)*. **Sep**

Musikfest Berlin

www.berlinerfestspiele.de

The world's top orchestras, including the Berliner Philharmoniker, present a series of concerts at the Philharmonie *(see p91)*. **Sep**

Art Forum Berlin

Messe Berlin • www.art-forum-berlin.com • 030 30 38 20 76

Creating a buzz since 1996, the Art Forum allows Berlin's most exciting contemporary art galleries to join forces with the hottest galleries from elsewhere in Europe and as far afield as the USA to show off their wares to the general public. **End Sep–early Oct**

JazzFest Berlin

Haus der Kulturen der Welt *(see p75)* & other venues www.berlinerfestspiele.de

Berlin's jazz festival has long been one of the most important on a continent loaded with such events. In recent years, the organizers have made an effort to expand the definition of "jazz" by bringing in acts some would think of as hip-hop, world music or rock. **Nov**

Berlin Christmas Markets

As elsewhere in Germany, every neighbourhood in Berlin hosts a Christmas market. Some are like funfairs, with Ferris wheels and entertainment. All have stalls

autumn and winter

selling seasonal German foods such as *Stollen* (fruit-bread), *Lebkuchen* (similar to gingerbread), *Glühwein* (like mulled wine) and stewed kale with *Pinkelwurst* sausage. You will also find traditional gifts and decorations such as the merry wooden figures made in Erzgebirge. Of particular note is the Christmas market at Gendarmenmarkt in Mitte (Map 5 D4), which, unlike the rest, has a small admission charge, but features top-notch entertainment and food from Berlin's best restaurants. **End Nov–Dec**

International Green Week
Messe Berlin • www.gruenewoche.com • 030 30 69 69 69

Green Week was introduced shortly after World War II, ostensibly as a forum for international food purveyors to do business with German shops and restaurants. From the start, though, ordinary citizens came in droves for the free samples – glasses of fresh, cold milk were a favourite. Today, there are fewer free samples, but a much larger array of foodstuffs from around the world, including many German regional specialities. **Mid-Jan**

Transmediale Germany
Haus der Kulturen der Welt *(see p75)*
www.transmediale.de • 030 24 74 97 61

Transmediale started as a challenging alternative to the Film Festival *(see below)* by showing avant-garde films, but it morphed into a festival of media art. Today, it is possibly the world's most important event in that genre, featuring a wide range of art-house videos, animations, Internet-based works and other digital productions. **Feb**

Berlin International Film Festival
Cinemas at Potsdamer Platz (Map 5 A5) & other locations
www.berlinale.de • 030 25 92 00

After Cannes, the "Berlinale" is arguably Europe's top film festival and includes European premieres of mainstream movies made in Hollywood. Golden and Silver Bears are awarded in various categories, such as Best Film and Outstanding Artistic Achievement. There are separate programmes for children's films, gay and lesbian cinema, documentaries and retrospectives of the work of celebrated directors and actors. **Feb**

Berlin enjoys one of Europe's best integrated mass transit systems. Its U-Bahn (metro trains) and S-Bahn (overland city trains), trams and buses cover virtually the whole city. There is no need for a car: savvy travellers take the subway or train to avoid traffic congestion. Numerous guided walking tours and traditional sightseeing bus tours are also available, and riverboats are a great way to explore the hidden corners of the German capital.

Arrival

Though Frankfurt am Main is Germany's main international airport hub, Berlin has two international airports of its own: Tegel and Schönefeld. (The regional airport, Tempelhof, is slated to close in 2010). Trains from other European cities arrive and depart at Berlin's grand new Hauptbahnhof train station. Some also stop at other railway stations in the city.

Tegel Airport

Tegel (TXL) is only 8 km (5 miles) northwest of Berlin's Charlottenburg district. Most foreign and domestic airlines, including inter-continental flights to New York (JFK and Newark) operated by Delta and Continental Airlines, arrive and depart here. A cab from the airport to the city will take 10 to 20 minutes, depending on the neighbourhood you are travelling to. Equally fast but cheaper are the buses TXL, 109 and X09, all of which stop on Kurfürstendamm in Charlottenburg.

Schönefeld Airport

Schönefeld (SXF) is located 19 km (12 miles) southeast of Berlin and caters mostly to budget or charter airlines and last-minute travellers. The S-bahn airport express takes only 30 minutes to Bahnhof Zoologischer

Garten. A cab is expensive in comparison with the train and takes 45 to 60 minutes to central Berlin.

By Train

Since 2006, all national and international trains arrive at and depart from the new, glitzy Hauptbahnhof-Lehrter Stadtbahnhof (Map 3 B3) in the government district. Some trains also stop at Wannsee, Spandau or Ostbahnhof. All of these railway stations offer direct transfers to U- and S-Bahn lines or buses.

By Car

Travellers approaching by road from the north or west usually enter Berlin's northern Reinickendorf district via the Berliner Ring, the city's autobahn beltway. From here, follow "Zentrum" signs, then signs either to Charlottenburg or Alexanderplatz in Mitte. Travellers from the south enter the city via the AVUS motorway.

Getting Around

Berlin's intricate network of U-Bahn and S-Bahn, Deutsche Bahn commuter trains, buses and trams is managed by the **Verkehrsverbund Berlin-Brandenburg (VBB)** and run by the **Berliner Verkehrsbetriebe (BVG)**. It is one of the largest and densest

public transportation systems in the world, and reasonably cheap to use.

Tickets and Fares

Fares depend on the time spent in the system and the zones travelled in, regardless of the means of transport. Most visitors remain in zone A, which covers most of Berlin, including the districts of Friedrichshain, Prenzlauer Berg and Kreuzberg. Zone B includes Grunewald and Dahlem. Zone C includes Potsdam.

Regular tickets start at just over €2 for two hours of unlimited travel in zones A and B. If you are travelling around for a whole day, a **Tageskarte** covers unlimited travel in zones A and B until 3am. **WelcomeCards** are good for 48 or 72 hours of unlimited travel and entitle visitors to discounts at sightseeing spots. The **7-Tages-Karte** offers seven days of unlimited travel.

Tickets can be purchased at counters and machines at stations. You must then insert the ticket into a validating machine to be stamped with the date and time just before you start your journey. Validating machines (usually small and red) are located in ticket halls, on platforms and on buses and trams. Buses and trams may also have ticket machines on board dispensing pre-validated tickets. (To avoid confusion on buses and trams, buy a Tageskarte and validate it at a station first.)

U-Bahn

With trains running at intervals of just two to four minutes, the underground U-Bahn is usually the fastest means of transport. There are 11 differently coloured lines, coded U1 to U15 (missing out numbers 10, 11, 13 and 14). Trains usually operate from 5am through to 1am the next morning or to 2am at weekends or during special events. On Friday and Saturday nights, U1, U9 and sections of most other lines operate through the whole night.

S-Bahn

The S-Bahn is the network of overground commuter and city trains. There are 15 lines connecting central Berlin with the suburbs, Potsdam and other Brandenburg towns. Trains run from 5am to 1am at 10- to 20-minute intervals. Most lines share tracks, so pay attention to the indicator boards.

Buses

Buses are separated into two systems: regular buses, which have two- or three-digit numbers and the final destination written at the front; and express M-bus lines, which stop only at major bus stations. One of the best ways to see the major landmarks of Berlin is to catch either a 100 or 200 double-decker bus, which run through Charlottenburg, the government district and Unter den Linden. The night bus service is extensive.

Trams

Trams operate in Mitte and other formerly East Berlin districts, with just one line extending into the formerly West Berlin district of Wedding. The main tram station is at Hackescher Markt (Map 6 E2). There are 27 lines, five of which run through the night.

Taxis

The official yellow cabs (usually Mercedes limousines) are safe, reliable and affordable. You can either call for one by phone or hail one on the street. If you are taking a cab for a distance of less than 2 km (1¼ miles), ask for the flat-rate Kurzstreckentarif (short-distance fare). Don't be bothered by the occasional rudeness from Berlin cab drivers.

Other Forms of Transport

In a city dominated by canals, rivers, and lakes, boat trips are immensely popular, and there are various ferry operators and stops (see p135). An unusual but fun way to explore central Berlin are the **Velotaxis**, which are like rickshaw bicycles with a passenger cabin in the back. These operate along Kurfürstendamm and Unter den Linden as well as at Potsdamer Platz and most sightseeing spots (from April to October only). Before you board a Velotaxi, make sure to negotiate the price first.

Tours

Berlin is a good place for walking tours, some of which are conducted in English. One of the best companies is **Berlin Walks**, which offers quirky, themed tours. **Stattreisen's** themed tours include Jewish history in Berlin and modern architecture, while **Art: berlin** is a trustworthy guide to the city's art scene. **Berlin Stadtrund-fahrtbüro** operates vintage double-decker buses on which you can take a one- to four-hour trip with guides who speak English and German.

Directory

Airport Information
(for both Tegel and Schönefeld)
0180 50 00 18 6
www.berlin-airport.de
Information in several languages

Art:berlin
030 28 09 63 90
www.artberlin-online.de

Berlin Stadtrundfahrtbüro
030 26 12 00 1
www.stadtrundfahrtbuero-berlin.de

Berlin Walks
030 30 19 19 4
www.berlinwalks.com
Meeting points at the taxi rank outside Zoologischer Garten and opposite Hackescher Markt S-Bahn station.

Berliner Verkehrsbetriebe (BVG)
030 19 44 9
www.bvg.de
Website information in German and English, including timetables, maps and journey planners.

Deutsche Bahn Commuter Trains
030 11 86 1
www.bahn.de

S-Bahn Berlin
030 29 74 33 33
www.s-bahn-berlin.de

Stattreisen
030 45 53 02 8
www.stattreisen.de

Taxis
030 26 20 26
030 21 01 01
030 21 02 02

Velotaxis
030 44 31 94 28
www.velotaxi.de

Verkehrsverbund Berlin-Brandenburg (VBB)
030 25 41 40
www.vbb-online.de
Information in several languages.

Berlin is a huge and complex city, and the information and tips given here will help you to enjoy a stress-free visit to the German capital. Some forward planning might be useful – start with the tourist information website, which also lists events. Visitors with special needs, such as wheelchair users, are supported by various associations and public services. Gay and lesbian travellers will also find a lot of support and things to do in this cosmopolitan city.

Disabled Travellers

Berlin's public transport system has excellent services for disabled travellers. Almost all U-Bahn and S-Bahn stations feature elevators, and buses have wheelchair access at street level. If you are in a wheelchair travelling by S- or U-Bahn, always approach the train's first carriage, and the driver will let you in via a special ramp. Restaurants, museums and official sightseeing spots are all supposed to provide wheelchair access – and, increasingly, they do.

Emergencies and Health

In the event of a serious accident or criminal incident, call 110 for the police. If there is a fire or medical emergency, call 112 for the fire service or ambulance. Emergency calls from any phone, including payphones and cell phones, are free. Visitors from EU countries are covered for emergency treatment. If you are a citizen of a non-EU country, make sure you have adequate medical cover on your travel insurance.

Hotlines for **Ärztenotdienst** (doctors) and **Zahnärztenotdienst** (dentists) can put you in touch with practitioners at short notice. Medicines are stocked at pharmacies (not in supermarkets). After 8pm, the **Apothekennotdienst** hotline can advise you where to find the nearest open pharmacy.

Gay and Lesbian Berlin

As Europe's unofficial gay and lesbian capital, Berlin has various scenes. The main hotspot is Schöneberg, but there are gay and lesbian places scattered throughout the city *(see p114)*. Many bars welcome a mixed crowd; some are for gay men only; very few are just for lesbians. The two leading gay magazines are *Siegessäule* and *Sergej* (the latter is distributed for free and caters to a younger readership). *L-mag* (**www.l-mag.de**) is a leading freebie for lesbians. A good preparation for a visit to Berlin are the websites **www.homo.net** and **www.gayromeo.de** with classified ads, destination guides and much more. The **Mann-o-meter** has a 24-hour helpline.

Listings/What's On

Berlin has several city magazines with articles and listings of movies, exhibitions, theatre shows, clubs and concerts. The oldest and biggest is *Tip* (online access via **www.berlinonline.de**), which caters to film buffs and art-lovers. *Zitty* (**www.zitty.de**) is less sleek but a very good resource for alternative and off-scene stage and other events. *Prinz* (**www.prinz.de**) and *[030]* (**www.berlino30.de**), as well as a series of smaller magazines such as *Kultur:news* (**www.kulturnews.de**), have a younger readership interested mainly in parties, clubs and music. *Kunstkalender* (**www.berliner-kunstkalender.de**) and *Artery Berlin* (not online) both list exhibitions throughout the year. The more conservative *Berlin Programm* (**www.berlin-programm.de**) features the most comprehensive listings.

Money

Most banks and various bureaux de change at the airport, railway stations and in the near vicinity of the Bahnhof Zoologischer Garten exchange US dollars and British sterling as well as other currencies for euros. US dollars are accepted in many fast-food restaurants, but rarely in shops. Credit cards, primarily MasterCard and Visa, are widely accepted, but smaller restaurants and shops do not take them. If your ATM card shows a Maestro, Eufiserv or Plus sign, you can withdraw cash with only a limited fee and also use them in chip-and-pin keypads in shops and restaurants.

Opening Hours

Most **shops** in Berlin open at 9 or 10am Monday to Saturday and close at 8pm, though smaller stores usually close earlier (between 4 and 6pm on weekdays and at 2, 4 or 6pm on Saturdays). **Post offices** are usually open from 8am to 6pm Monday to Friday and 8am to 1 or 2pm on Saturday. The post office on

Joachimsthaler Strasse (Map 8 F2) at the Neues Kranzler Eck has extended opening hours (8am–10pm daily). **Banks** usually open at 9 or 10am and close at 6pm. Many banks have one or two days with earlier closing hours (usually Wednesday or Friday afternoon at 3pm). Banks are closed on Saturday. All shops, banks and post offices are closed on Sunday and over public holidays.

As there is no official closing hour in Berlin, restaurants, bars and clubs can stay open throughout the night. **Restaurants** are busiest between 7 and 10pm, and often close at midnight. Most **pubs** and **bars** do not even have official closing times, but are open until the last patrons have enjoyed their last drinks. **Nightclubs** may even stay open until 4 or 5am.

Phones and Communications

Public phones can be found all over the city and are usually operated with phone cards (*Telefonkarten*), available at newsstands and shops, or euro coins. A few phone booths at popular sightseeing areas (for example, on Ku'damm) also accept credit cards.

Mobile phones operate at GSM 900 MHz or 1800 MHz frequency bands. Visitors from the US or Canada will need a tri-band phone to connect with German networks. There are many Internet cafés dotted around the city, and the **easyInternetcafé** chain has a huge outlet on Kurfürstendamm. In some areas, such as in the Sony Center and at places on Ku'damm, public Wireless LAN is offered for free.

Security

Berlin is one of the safest large cities in the world. However, as in any tourist destination, you should observe some basic rules. Watch your wallet and purse or handbag in any crowded area such as on public transport or when sitting at an outdoor café table. Pickpocketing is still known, mostly at bus exits. Be alert when using ATM machines, as they have been targets of various scams, and make sure that nobody is standing behind you when you key in your PIN. If you are openly gay or have a dark complexion, avoid late-night train, tram or U-Bahn rides through Friedrichshain and other eastern districts as well as Brandenburg.

Tipping

As a rule, if service has been good, give 5 to 10 per cent to waiters (in Germany, bar and restaurant bills never include a service charge), bartenders, hairdressers, beauty therapists and taxi drivers. It is considered impolite to directly tip the owner or boss, however. Cab drivers are often satisfied if you simply round up your fare to the full euro amount.

Tourist Information

Berlin's official tourist organization is the **Berlin Tourismus Marketing GmbH**, which has two great websites in various languages. These offer accommodation booking services and tickets for shows *(see also p91)*. There are tourist offices at Tegel airport, Europa-Center and the Brandenburger Tor.

(see also p91)

Directory

Advice for Foreign Nationals
030 90 17 23 9

Ambulance Service
112

Apothekennotdienst
(pharmacy emergency service)
030 31 00 31

Ärtzenotdienst
(doctors on call)
030 31 00 31

Berlin Association for the Disabled
030 20 43 84 7 (noon–5pm Wed)
www.bbv-ev.de

Berlin Tourismus Marketing GmbH
030 25 00 25
www.berlin.de • www.btm.de

easyInternetcafé
Kurfürstendamm 224,
Charlottenburg (Map 8 E2)
Open 6:30am–2am
www.easyeverything.com

Fire Service
112

German Red Cross
030 85 00 55

Maneo
(violence against gays)
030 21 63 33 6 (5–7 pm daily)
www.maneo.de

Mann-o-Meter
Bülowstr. 106
030 21 68 00 8
www.mann-o-meter.de

Police
110

Potsdam Tourist Information
0331 27 55 80
www.potsdam.de

Zahnärztenotdienst
(emergency dentists)
030 89 00 43 33
www.kzv-berlin.de

restaurants

Berlin's gastronomic scene runs late into the night and includes many ethnic restaurants – notably Turkish places – and creative fusion restaurants alongside classic German establishments. There may be fewer high-powered, Michelin-starred kitchens in Berlin than in some other German cities, but nowhere else in the country will you find such a diverse range of restaurants offering generally low-priced, yet high-quality food.

RESTAURANTS

Berlin's dining scene has never been more diverse and creative. The range of cuisines is truly international, but one of the most exciting developments is the reinvention of traditional German recipes by the city's young chefs. Among the best for this type of cuisine are Hugo's *(see p35)* and Haus Berlin *(see p44)*. Zoe *(see p33)* takes things further with a hybrid of German and Asian flavours, while Facil *(see p34)* creatively mixes French and German cooking styles.

Jürgen Scheunemann

Best German Home Cooking

Traditional home cooking should be enjoyed in a rustic setting such as the **Altes Zollhaus** *(see p42)*, a half-timbered house. Hearty Bavarian and Franconian treats are dished up at the **Engelbecken** and the **Florian** *(see p40 for both)*, while Berlin's oldest pub, **Zur Letzten Instanz** *(see p33)*, has served pork knuckle and beer since 1621.

Gourmet Dining

For an unforgettable romantic dinner with a view of the glittering city lights, book at **Hugo's** *(see p35)*, Berlin's hottest gourmet restaurant. Another Michelin-starred temple of good taste is **Facil** *(see p34)*, which serves French-German fusion cuisine. For Asian gourmet food, head to **Kuchi** *(see p37)*, the city's trendiest Japanese restaurant.

Style Statements

Berlin's hip designer restaurant scene is dominated by two places: **Bocca di Bacco** *(see p29)*, a high-class Italian restaurant that's popular with movie stars; and **Vox** *(see p35)*, a coolly understated Asian restaurant. A more traditionally form of elegance can be enjoyed at the **Remise im Schloss Klein-Glienicke** *(see p43)*.

choice eats

Fusion Cuisine

One of the few authentic fusion cuisine restaurants is **Oktogon Fusion** *(see p33)*, where you can sample dishes with roots in China, Turkey, France and India. Minimalist **Pan Asia** *(see p31)* draws on culinary influences from across Asia, with a focus on healthy, organic food. French brasserie **Borchardt** *(see p28)* caters to the jet set.

Turkish Restaurants

Berlin is proud of its Turkish contingent, and the doner kebab has become one of the city's signature dishes. The premier and most creative Turkish restaurant is **Defne** *(see p42)*, a Kreuzberg institution thanks to its light, modern versions of Turkish meat and fish dishes. The **Hasir** *(see p41)* eateries offer tasty down-to-earth fare.

Budget Eateries

Healthy and fresh produce is turned into delicious Asian soups and salads at **Monsieur Vuong** *(see p32)* and into great sandwiches and bagels at the **Bagel-Station** *(see p30)*. Buzzing **Ali Baba** *(see p36)* – a pizza hangout that's popular with students, backpackers and other young travellers – is fun for a late-night bite.

Borchardt *VIP-studded brasserie*   **5 C4**

Französische Strasse 47, Mitte • 030 81 88 62 30
>> www.gastart.de Open 11:30am–2am daily

A supremely popular French brasserie located in Mitte (formerly East Berlin), Borchardt can trace its origins back to 1853, when August F W Borchardt worked as caterer to the royal court. The restaurant itself was created after World War II, when its high-ceilinged dining room seemed a stark contrast to the typically dark and dingy Berlin eating places of the time. Revamped after the fall of the Wall, it rapidly drew custom away from the high-class haunts of western Berlin and became a symbol of the newly reunited city, a reputation further enhanced when Hollywood stars began to include it on their European itineraries.

Today, Borchardt's fame is underpinned partly by the food itself, which qualifies as solid French cooking, and partly by the beautiful Art Nouveau setting, but most of all by the high-powered ambience. The patrons – many of them politicians – create a lively atmosphere. On any given night, you might spot supermodel Claudia Schiffer sitting with friends in one corner while high-ranking politicians butter up their allies in another. But there is an air of nonchalance too: Borchardt doesn't shout about its credentials, and guests know they can generally enjoy dinner undisturbed by other diners or the paparazzi.

The dining room is a stunning, meticulously restored Wilhelmine-era hall, complete with dark marble columns and heavy leather furniture. Pride of place goes to a mosaic mural dating from the 19th century.

The menu has all the French classics, including a good steak with French fries. Japanese Kobe beef sometimes makes an appearance, as does white asparagus, and Wiener schnitzel with a warm potato salad. In summer, Borchardt's courtyard is one of Berlin's loveliest dining spots. A reservation is essential if you want to dine in the evening. If you can't get a booking for supper, try for a late lunch, when tables are usually available. **Expensive**

Lutter & Wegner *Austrian schnitzel*   `5 D4`

Charlottenstrasse 56, Mitte • 030 20 29 54 0
» www.l-w-berlin.de Open 11am–3am daily

German Sekt (the Teutonic answer to French bubbly) was first made in 1811 in a historic city mansion now occupied by Lutter & Wegner. Today, you can enjoy Sekt in the adjoining wine bar (order the light Riesling Sekt, sold exclusively here), then dine on delicious Austrian food in the restaurant. The dining room, with its high ceilings, wood panels and parquet floor, is a suitably elegant venue for the rich and beautiful. Many patrons are classical music buffs who cross the street from the concert hall opposite.

The house speciality is an enormous Wiener schnitzel (undoubtedly the best in town), served as it should be – with just a warm potato salad and a lemon. The *Sauerbraten* (sour roast) and Hungarian goulash with *Spätzle* (a cross between noodles and dumplings) are also popular. The set meals are particularly good value. Reservations are a must after 8pm. **Moderate**

Bocca di Bacco *blockbuster Italian*   `5 C4`

Friedrichstrasse 167–8, Mitte • 030 20 67 28 28
» www.boccadibacco.de
Open noon–midnight Mon–Sat, 6pm–midnight Sun

After film premieres in town, the stars of Hollywood (Tom Hanks, Jodie Foster, Tom Cruise et al) join the other glamorous diners here for high-class Italian meals. The original Bocca is one of western Berlin's oldest and most authentic Italian restaurants. This branch serves creative Tuscan food and a huge selection of Italian wines, and it is consistently ranked among Berlin's very best restaurants.

Chef Luriano Mura has scored high on the Gault Millau rating system with some of the best pasta and fresh fish dishes outside Italy. His grilled sea bream in a potato wrap, and ravioli filled with sea bass are legendary. The dining room is stylish, with graphic works of art on the walls, and the service is smooth. In summer, you can relax at one of the long communal tables outside. **Expensive**

» *Cheap: under €8 for a main course; moderate: €8–15; expensive: over €15*   `29`

Margaux international gourmet dining `5 B3`

Unter den Linden 78, Mitte • 030 22 65 26 11
>> www.margaux-berlin.de
Open 7–10:30pm Mon–Thu, noon–2pm & 7–10:30pm Fri & Sat

When it first opened, Margaux aspired to be Berlin's most luxurious restaurant, but it soon went bankrupt. Then the original chef, Michael Hoffmann, bought the place and lowered the prices. His creative international cooking has now earned him a Michelin star. **Expensive**

Vau German excellence `5 D4`

Jägerstrasse 54–5, Mitte • 030 20 29 73 0
>> www.vau-berlin.de Open noon–2:30 & 7–10:30pm Mon–Sat

One of Berlin's longest-running gourmet restaurants, Vau still holds its own among excellent newcomers. Chef Kolja Kleeberg excels at traditional German game and fish dishes, which are beautifully presented on the plate. Menus are seasonal and have included luxury ingredients such as caviar. **Expensive**

Bagel-Station Brötchen with a hole `6 F1`

Rosenthaler Strasse 49, Mitte • 030 93 95 75 00
>> www.bagelstation.com Open 8am–8pm
Sat–Wed (to 6pm Sun), 8am–midnight Thu & Fri

Though many Germans still see the bagel as simply a *Brötchen* (bread roll) with a peculiar hole in the middle, others appreciate its true character. Bagel-Station is the city's best bagel bakery, where they are prepared fresh with classic toppings. **Cheap**

Breakfast in Berlin

In a city full of *Lebenkünstler* – people who never seem to work – taking a leisurely breakfast is a popular pastime. Alongside the breakfast buffets and brunches that feature in the grand hotels, Berlin is known for its **Frühstückscafés**. **Café Savigny** (see p126) and **Café Einstein** (see pp124 & 135) are the most sophisticated places to enjoy eggs, salmon and *Brötchen* with a glass of sparkling wine. In Kreuzberg, **Café am Ufer** (see p129) and the **Freischwimmer** (Map 11 A4, Schlesisches Tor 2a, www.freischwimmer-berlin.de) overlook the Landwehrkanal and offer international breakfasts. In Mitte, grab an American breakfast at **Barcomi's Deli** (Map 6 E1, Sophienstrasse 21), or ransack the buffet at the historic **Opernpalais** (see p124).

Hackescher Hof *solid German food*

6 F1

Rosenthaler Strasse 40–41, Mitte • 030 28 35 29 3
>> www.hackescher-hof.de
Open 7am–2am Mon–Fri, 9am–2am Sat & Sun

Hackescher Hof's icon of a walking man comes from the East German traffic signals and has become a symbol of East Germany. (On the West German traffic lights, by contrast, the signalman seems bored with his job.) The restaurant has a wonderful location at the entrance to the historic Hackesche Höfe courtyards *(see p125)*. You can dine outside in the first, most beautiful, courtyard, or choose the huge dining room with its high ceilings and dark wood furnishings lit by spotlights and chandeliers.

The food is mostly traditional German fare, with some Italian and French accents. The kitchen is open from breakfast right through to the early hours of the morning. The lunch menu (noon–4pm Mon–Fri) is an excellent deal; the main dinner menu kicks in at 6pm. Booking is advisable in the evening. **Moderate**

Pan Asia *Asian smoothies*

6 F1

Rosenthaler Strasse 38, Mitte • 030 27 90 88 11
>> www.panasia.de
Open noon–midnight daily (to 1am Fri & Sat)

Located near the Hackesche Höfe, Pan Asia's ultra-minimalist dining hall looks like a designer's idea of a basic 1970s cafeteria. The mostly young and hip guests usually don't mind sharing long, wooden tables and benches, but those not up to the spirit of togetherness can be seated at individual tables.

Service is not very reliable, and you may have a long wait for a seat and then your meal. But the food itself is the focus at Pan Asia (which explains why the room contains little to distract diners) and, in terms of healthy eating, the experience is wonderful. Dishes hailing from Vietnam, Thailand and China are carefully steamed or grilled, rather than boiled or fried, and are all the better for having no trace of butter, cream or non-organic fat. Sushi is available, too (though not Berlin's best). **Moderate**

Restaurants

Schwarzenraben *pasta and more* `6 F1`
Neue Schönhauser Strasse 13, Mitte • 030 28 39 16 98
≫ www.schwarzenraben.de Café open 11:30am–midnight
daily; restaurant 6:30pm–2am

One of the most popular places in Mitte, Schwarzenraben has a colourful past. Its narrow, arcaded dining
hall dates from the 1890s, when it was a soup kitchen
for the destitute. Around the time of World War I, the
place decayed into one of the city's most seedy bars;
in the 1920s it was shut down and used as a movie
theatre for poor people. Today it is a place where
entrepreneurs and artists partake of pizza and pasta.

The Italian cooking may not offer any surprises, but
the pasta is masterfully executed, and there are six
risotto creations, some of which use seasonal local
ingredients such as white asparagus. Lunchtime
(noon–6pm) features "BancoEspressoPasta", in which
pasta dishes are prepared in front of guests. Alterna-
tives include grilled tuna on a sun-dried tomato
pesto sauce with mashed potatoes. **Expensive**

Monsieur Vuong *Vietnamese for beginners* `6 F1`
Alte Schönhauser Strasse 46, Mitte • 030 30 87 26 43
≫ www.monsieurvuong.de
Open noon–midnight Mon–Sat, 2pm–midnight Sun

Until recently known only to insiders, this tiny
Vietnamese joint is now one of the most popular
restaurants with the young, stylish Mitte crowd.
The menu of light dishes from Saigon and the Mekong
Delta changes every two days and features many
excellent soups and snacks. Meals are inexpensive
and quickly prepared to order. Guests are seated at
separate tables or on small bamboo chairs crammed
behind a curved counter. Red walls, Buddha images
and fish swimming in an aquarium guarantee a
peaceful state of mind. Monsieur Vuong – the
muscular young man immortalized in a black-and-
white photograph in the restaurant – is the father of
the owner, chef Doug Vuong. You may have to stand
in line to grab lunch or dinner here (no reservations
are accepted), but it's worth the wait. **Cheap**

Café Orange *neighbourhood hangout* `5 D1`

Oranienburger Strasse 32, Mitte • 030 28 38 52 42

Open 9am–midnight Mon–Fri, 9am–2am Sat & Sun

Café Orange has been a fixture in the Scheunenviertel since the area turned fashionable in the 1990s, and it still holds on to a slightly off-beat charm. This is a great place for breakfast or, indeed, for a German or Italian snack any time of the day or half the night. Sit outside and watch the world go by. **Cheap**

Zoe *nouvelle German-Asian fusion food* `6 F2`

Rochstrasse 1, Mitte • 030 24 04 56 35

>> www.zoe-berlin.de Open noon–midnight Mon–Fri, 6pm–midnight Sat, 2–10pm Sun

With a German and a Malaysian chef working side by side, Zoe manages a successful fusion of two very different cuisines. The menu changes daily but always includes a roasted, pan-fried or deep-fried concoction, served with noodles and mushrooms. **Moderate**

Zur Letzten Instanz *hearty Berlin food* `6 G3`

Waisenstrasse 14–16, Mitte • 030 24 25 52 8

>> www.zurletzteninstanz.de Open noon–1am daily

Berlin's oldest restaurant and pub opened in 1621 in a tiny, cobblestoned alleyway near the town hall. Sidestepped by history, this charming place serves old-fashioned dishes such as *Eisbein* (pork knuckle) and *Rinderroulade* (a beef dish) to accompany your beer. It's a great way to mingle with the locals. **Cheap**

Oktogon Fusion *gourmet globalism* `5 A5`

Leipziger Platz 10, Tiergarten • 030 20 64 28 64

>> www.oktogon-berlin.de

Open noon–midnight Mon–Fri, 6pm–midnight Sat & Sun

The menu at Berlin's best fusion cuisine restaurant reads like a trip around the world: dim sum from China, felafels from Turkey, exotic French quails with lentils from India, Scottish salmon in a Thai marinade. They're reasonably priced for the quality. **Expensive**

Facil *international gourmet cuisine* `5 A5`

Potsdamer Strasse 3 (at The Mandala Hotel), Tiergarten
030 59 00 51 23 4
» www.facil.de Open noon–3pm & 7–11pm Mon–Fri

The art of fine dining is celebrated night after night at Facil. This Michelin-starred gem is set discreetly on an upper floor of The Mandala Hotel *(see p153)*, far from the crowded city streets. The light-filled dining room is ideal for a quiet business lunch, but there is more atmosphere in the evening, when patrons can enjoy a romantic, candlelit dinner.

The spacious room features a glistening Italian Giallo Reale marble floor, mahogany panels and Italian Iguzzini lamps. A retractable glass roof and enticing Japanese garden are the surprising features, while the last word in style has to be the petite cushioned chairs for ladies' handbags at each table. The service is impeccable and unobtrusive, and yet less stiff than in many other Michelin-starred restaurants. Entrust your palate to sommelier Felix Voges, who will recommend a different wine for each course and explain how they complement the dishes.

The cuisine itself is best exemplified by the changing six-course dinner menu with imaginative French and German dishes. The price of this is fixed and makes Facil the most affordable of the German Michelin-starred restaurants (and, in turn, one of the most popular, making reservations essential). Creations such as Dover sole filled with lobster and served on roasted cauliflower, or roebuck on peppered cherries and celery, are works of art – and their appreciation takes up a full evening.

The mastermind behind this choreography of dishes that tantalize the tongue and eye is Michael Kempf. Born in 1977, he is one of the youngest first-rate chefs in Germany. Kempf plays creatively with traditional German, French and Mediterranean recipes, minimizing the number of ingredients for each, and he succeeds in making the enjoyment of food a pure and simple one. **Expensive**

Vox *show kitchen in a top-class hotel* 9 B1

Marlene-Dietrich-Platz 2 (at Grand Hyatt Hotel), Tiergarten
»» www.berlin.grand.hyatt.com • 030 25 53 17 72
Open noon–2:30pm & 6:30–midnight Mon–Fri, 6:30–midnight
Sat, 6:30am–2pm & 6:30pm–midnight Sun

The Grand Hyatt's opening in 1999 heralded Berlin's
coming of age as a new metropolis. The name of the
hotel's restaurant, Vox, harks back to the "roaring
20s" – a decade when the Vox radio station and
amusement temple entertained visitors at this
location. Still the playground of big city hotshots,
the new Vox sets a tone that speaks of power with its
dark woods and furniture designed by Hannes
Wettstein. The neighbouring bar also has a decadent
setting with black leather seating and red walls.

The Asian-inspired international cuisine is prepared
with gusto in an open show kitchen, with an emphasis
on sushi and French-Italian creations. Live jazz is a
nightly draw, but if dinner is booked up, come for the
great value two-course lunch. **Expensive**

Hugo's *dinner with a view* 8 G1

Budapester Strasse 2 (at InterContinental Hotel), Tiergarten
030 26 02 12 63
»» www.hugos-restaurant.de Open 6–10:30pm Mon–Sat

Voted the best German restaurant in 2003 by the
country's leading gourmet magazine, Hugo's has
brought a fresh approach to fine dining. The Michelin-
starred establishment is set on the top floor of
the InterContinental Hotel *(see p151)*, from where
it has views to the high-rises of Potsdamer Platz.
Reservations are nearly always necessary for dinner,
with a waiting list of up to two weeks.

The beaming couples and businesspeople dining
here are treated to no-nonsense German cuisine,
masterfully prepared by Thomas Kammeier, one of
Berlin's shooting stars of the pots and saucepans.
He and his team rely on only the best locally grown
produce for their hearty meat and fish creations. Try
lamb with ramsons (a type of garlic) or crispy grilled
pike-perch with risotto and candied olives. **Expensive**

Ali Baba *pizza to go*
8 E2

Bleibtreustrasse 45, Charlottenburg • 030 88 11 35 0
Open 11am–3am daily

This *Imbiss* (food kiosk) is thronged at night with students and backpackers. Order slices of spicy pizza – salami or cheese – from the street counter, or step inside the small, characterful restaurant for a wider choice of food. The *moules frites* (mussels and french fries) are a must in summer. **Cheap**

XII Apostel *heavenly pizza*
8 E2

Bleibtreustrasse 49, Charlottenburg • 030 31 21 43 3
➤➤ www.12-apostel.de Open 24 hours

One of the trendiest (and noisiest) Italians in town, XII Apostel is a slightly ironic version of the traditional pizzeria, complete with fake plaster sculptures and kitsch frescoes. The enormous pizzas are named after the 12 apostles. "Judas" is a spicy combination of mozzarella, salami and pepperoni. **Moderate**

Deli 31 *subs and salads*
8 E2

Bleibtreustrasse 31, Charlottenburg • 030 88 47 46 02
➤➤ www.bleibtreu.com
Open 8am–9pm daily (to 8pm Sun)

Part of the Hotel Bleibtreu *(see p153)*, Deli 31's modern interior is as chic as its clientele. You can sit at street-side tables, but the best seats are at the counter, where chefs excel at small talk while preparing bagels, sandwiches and soups. **Cheap**

Berlin's Traditional Dishes

For centuries, Berlin was mainly a working-class city, whose population needed plenty of carbohydrates, especially during the long, ghastly winters. The typical Berliner would guzzle down his daily pork knuckle with sauerkraut and mashed split-peas, or treat himself to *Casseler Nacken* (smoked pork chops – a creation of 19th-century Berlin butcher Herr Cassel) with mashed potatoes, or fried liver, onions and apple rings. These days, young chefs offer lighter versions of the classics. The good old, fat *Currywurst* hasn't changed, though. This concoction of *Bratwurst* sausage in a curried tomato and paprika sauce emerged in the days of scarceness and odd leftovers following World War II. It is sold at *Imbisse* (fast-food stalls).

Kuchi *trendy sushi place*   7 D1

Kantstrasse 30, Charlottenburg • 030 31 50 78 15
Also at Gipsstrasse 3, Mitte • 030 28 38 66 22
>> www.kuchi.de
Open noon–midnight Mon–Sat, 6pm–midnight Sun

Kuchi started a new trend in Germany with its hip Asian cuisine and is still the talk of the town thanks to its consistently high quality of sushi and other Japanese dishes, an inviting lounge atmosphere and a devoted crowd of regulars.

The two Japanese brothers who own Kuchi have opened a takeaway service next door (called Next to Kuchi) and a second restaurant in Mitte, which is equally popular. However, the tiny, original restaurant is still the heart and soul of their little sushi empire. It's decorated with plain wood panels and some bamboo fittings. Vaguely modern lampshades hang over the sushi bar, and the room has a hushed ambience. Diners can choose to sit at the bar or join others at long tables. The latest fusion, electronic and lounge music plays while Kuchi's patrons sample sushi, sashimi, ingenious inside-out sushi rolls, soups and other creations including a sprinkling of Chinese and Thai recipes.

A speciality rarely found in other Japanese restaurants in Germany is the barbecued *yaki* – skewers with beef, pork, fish or shiitake mushrooms. Try the *yaki-sepia* with tiny octopus pieces or order the sampler of five different *yaki*, which comes with a free bowl of rice and *kimchi* (pickled cabbage). For a new twist on sushi, order the tuna or salmon crunchy plate: it certainly is sushi, but hidden in a deep-fried coat and often described as Japanese-style Kentucky Fried Chicken (don't let that put you off). **Moderate**

Restaurants

Florian *Franconian nouvelle cuisine* `8 E1`
Grolmanstrasse 52, Charlottenburg • 030 31 39 18 4
>> www.rflo.de Open 6pm–3am daily

Florian-owners Gerti and Ute are like tough but caring mothers to the arty Charlottenburg crowd. Actors, directors and writers enjoy their high-standard Franconian classics such as *Nürnberger Rostbratwürstchen* (sausage) or *Maultaschen*, the southern German version of ravioli. **Moderate**

Mar y Sol *high-quality tapas* `8 E1`
Savignyplatz 5, Charlottenburg • 030 31 32 59 3
Open 11:30am–1am daily

A sleek, upbeat version of a traditional Spanish *tapas* bar, Mar y Sol is a real delight in summer, with its leafy, Mediterranean-style patio and fountain. (The dining room is quite dark.) The *tapas* sampler is a good choice from the huge selection on the menu, and the fresh fish dishes are excellent. **Moderate**

Engelbecken *basic Bavarian* `7 B1`
Witzlebenstrasse 31 • 030 61 52 81 0, Charlottenburg
>> www.engelbecken.de ✓
Open 4pm–1am Mon–Sat, noon–1am Sun

Worlds apart from the hip restaurants, Engelbecken has a simple dining room with basic furniture. The big draw is the hearty Bavarian food, including pork knuckle with sauerkraut, hot sausages, schnitzel and, when in season, white asparagus. **Cheap**

Turkish Street Food

The *Döner* is Berlin's new signature dish. These days, Berliners and the city's 150,000 Turks consume even more of these bread pockets filled with lamb or chicken meat, salad and goat's cheese than they do of the beloved *Currywurst* (see p36). This is partly because *Döner* is cheaper than *Currywurst* (as little as 99 cents). It is also less stodgy than that famously calorie-laden sausage in a greasy tomato sauce. Food outlets known as *Dönerbuden* or *Dönerimbisse* can be found at every street corner. As well as the ubiquitous *Döner*, these offer Turkish pizza, pastry *Börek* and Turkish tea. Some of the best Turkish snack stands are the colourful **Hasir** branches found across the city (see opposite).

Hasir *authentic Turkish food*

`10 G2`

Adalbertstrasse 10, Kreuzberg • 030 61 42 37 3
>> www.hasir.de Open 24 hours ✓

The Hasir family's empire caters to the Berliners' enthusiastic adoption of authentic Turkish food. Of the various Hasir branches in the city, the new and fancier ones are quite nice, but the original restaurant is the most homely. Located in Kreuzberg, which is home to a large proportion of Berlin's Turkish community, this first Hasir feels halfway between a *Dönerimbiss (see box opposite)* and a genuine restaurant. However, the warm hospitality and heavenly dishes quickly transport diners to Istanbul.

On the menu are char-grilled meat and fish dishes, soups, pies, Turkish pizzas and pastas, potatoes and many vegetarian choices. Here, too, is the ultimate Kreuzberg doner kebab, roasting on an upright spit. The clientele is typical of the neighbourhood: an eclectic mixture of local kids, students, ageing hippies, Turks and Germans. **Cheap**

E.T.A. Hoffmann *affordable gourmet*

`9 C4`

Yorckstrasse 83, Kreuzberg • 030 78 09 88 09
>> www.restaurant-e-t-a-hoffmann.de ✓
Open 5pm–1am Wed–Mon

Named after the German romantic poet who is laid to rest off Mehringdamm, around the corner, the E.T.A. Hoffmann restaurant is a tranquil, dignified retreat from the harder edges of Kreuzberg. The dining room's high ceilings and simple, functional oak furniture create a look of understated elegance.

The kitchen offers Alsatian, French and German Baden cuisine. Chef Thomas Kurt has cooked his way up to Michelin stardom elsewhere and offers that quality here but without the affectations and at unbeatable prices. Light fish dishes such as pike or catfish, accented with carefully composed sauces and vegetables, are signature dishes in summer; you can tuck into more hearty German fare in winter. Everything is prepared with little fuss, using fresh local produce and dashes of modern flair. **Moderate**

>> *Try German wines: they are cheaper than their French or Italian counterparts and usually of a high quality*

Defne *stylish and Turkish* `10 G3`
Planufer 92c, Kreuzberg • 030 81 79 71 11
>> www.defne-restaurant.de
Open 4pm–midnight daily, also 10am–3pm Sun

Defne (Turkish for "laurel") opened in 2003 and quickly became one of Berlin's top Turkish joints. On the menu are modernized versions of Turkish meat and fish dishes, and a good choice for vegetarians. The garden overlooks a canal. **Cheap**

Sale e Tabacchi *dependable Italian* `9 D1`
Kochstrasse 18, Kreuzberg • 030 25 21 15 5
Open noon–3pm & 6pm–1am daily

A classic Italian trattoria, Sale e Tabacchi is frequented by journalists and artists working next door at the cheeky left-wing daily *Tageszeitung*. The media crowd's gossipy chatter rises above the dependable pasta, meat and fish dishes in a high-ceilinged dining room and lovely courtyard. **Moderate**

Altes Zollhaus *gourmet duck dish* `10 E3`
Carl-Herz-Ufer 30, Kreuzberg • 030 69 23 30 0
>> www.altes-zollhaus.com Open 6pm–1am Tue–Sat

Set in a historic customs house on the picturesque bank of the Landwehrkanal, Altes Zollhaus is an island of gourmet German cuisine in Kreuzberg. The signature dish that made chef Herbert Beltle famous is his crispy country duck, slowly oven-roasted and filled with apples, raisins and onions. **Expensive**

Mutter *international home-cooking* `8 H3`
Hohenstaufenstrasse 4, Schöneberg • 030 21 64 99 0
Open 10am–3am daily

Given its huge portions and popularity with students, Mutter (German for "mother") is, indeed, a homely restaurant. A fixture of the off-beat Schöneberg scene, it serves cool Caribbean drinks and an eclectic mix of Italian and Asian dishes, including delectable glass noodle salads. Reserve an outdoor table. **Moderate**

Diekmann im Châlet Suisse *Swiss hospitality*

Clayallee 99, Grunewald • 030 83 26 36 2 • ⑤ Grunewald
>> www.j-diekmann.de Open 11:30am–10pm daily

This little hut in the thick woods of the Grunewald
feels like a Swiss Alpine retreat and is a popular
destination in summer. Traditional Berlin food is
barbecued in the beer garden, while Swiss classics
such as veal with *rösti* (fried potato cakes) add
another dimension to the menu. **Expensive**

Forsthaus Paulsborn *a true Berlin experience*

Hüttenweg 90, Grunewald • 030 81 81 91 0 • ⑤ Grunewald
>> www.forsthaus-paulsborn.de Open 9am–11pm Tue–Sun

The most popular restaurant in Grunewald is located
in a historic mansion with a terrace in the middle of
the woods. The hearty food is traditional German.
Game dishes are a must in winter, while local
freshwater fish dishes and charcoal-barbecued meat
creations are just right in summer. **Moderate**

Remise im Schloss
Klein-Glienicke *Prussian elegance*

Königstrasse 36, Wannsee • 030 80 54 00 0 • ⑤ Wannsee
>> www.schloss-glienicke.de Open noon–9:30pm Wed–Sun

If you ever wanted to wine and dine like a Prussian
king, this is the place to do so. The restaurant is set
in the Palace of Klein-Glienicke on the Wannsee lake,
built in the mid-19th century by architect Carl Friedrich
Schinkel and landscaper Peter Joseph Lenné. Franz
Raneburger, one of Germany's few top-rated chefs to
have lived through many vogues of gourmet cuisine,
composes first-class, yet low-key, regional dishes
with an emphasis on fresh ingredients. Char fish with
leaf-spinach, or angler-fish with braised tomatoes,
and the occasional local meat dishes such as Müritz
lamb with green beans and oven-roasted potatoes,
are unforgettable. Ask about concerts and cultural
events at the palace when reserving a table. If dinner
is booked up, the low-priced two-course lunch
(noon–3pm Wed–Fri) is a great alternative. **Expensive**

Restaurants

Juliette *cosy French restaurant*

Jägerstrasse 39, Potsdam • 0331 27 01 79 1 • ⑤ Potsdam
>> www.restaurant-juliette.de Open noon–10pm daily

Set in a half-timbered house in Potsdam, this charming little restaurant evokes French Huguenot style. Service, while sometimes slow, is dedicated. Set menus of high-quality French cuisine include light salads and seafood courses. Sit at the back, in sight of the open fireplace, where it's quiet. **Expensive**

Haus Berlin *modern German cooking* `4 H4`

Strausberger Platz 1, Friedrichshain • 030 24 25 60 8
>> www.haus-berlin.net Open 11:30am–midnight daily

A 1950s Stalinist high-rise is the location of an establishment that has helped to revive a dull neighbourhood. Rüdiger Uentz's team serves light, modern versions of Berlin classics such as pork knuckle with sauerkraut and parsley potatoes, and chanterelle mushroom dishes in summer. **Moderate**

Noiquattro *Italian for East Berliners* `4 H4`

Strausberger Platz 2, Friedrichshain • 030 24 04 56 22
>> www.noiquattro.de
Open noon–midnight Mon–Sat

The walls of Noiquattro are paler than any in Charlottenburg, and the artworks are more abstract than in Wilmersdorf. The cooking, too, is fresher and more daring. A typical meal might be spring chicken on berry risotto, followed by apricot strudel. **Moderate**

Gugelhof *French cooking fit for presidents* `4 G2`

Knaackstrasse 37, Prenzlauer Berg • 030 44 29 22 9
>> www.gugelhof.com
Open 4pm–11:30pm Mon–Fri, 10am–11:30pm Sat & Sun

Bill Clinton ate at this French/Swiss restaurant in 2000, and it's been buzzing ever since. The calorie-rich food includes *Raclette* (Swiss cheese fondue), *Flamme-kuchen* (Alsatian pizza) and *Choucroute* (cabbage, blood sausage and mashed potatoes). **Moderate**

Southwest, East & North

Pasternak *Russian home from home* `4 G2`

Knaackstrasse 22–4, Prenzlauer Berg • 030 44 13 39 9
>> www.restaurant-pasternak.de
Open 10am–1am daily

In a city with more than 200,000 Russians, Pasternak is a place for homesick Russian souls who want to forget the grim German reality over a good glass of vodka, some spicy, dark red beetroot borscht soup and heart-breaking folk music. The restaurant, set in a historic tenement house, opened shortly after German reunification in 1990 and was soon a favourite among not only Russians but also the East German intellectual elite, who had learned Russian in school.

The Socialist days of shortage are gone, but the menu limits itself to a few Russian dishes such as beef stroganoff, *Scharkoje* (lamb stew with onions, potatoes and vegetables), a mixed fish grill plate, and caviar that is correctly served on ice with a blini (Russian pancake) and whipped cream. Vodka or the Russian beer on tap go with any meal here. **Moderate**

Drei *sustenance for world travellers* `4 F1`

Lychener Strasse 30, Prenzlauer Berg • 030 41 71 57 18
>> www.restaurant-drei.de
Open 6pm–midnight daily, also 10am–4pm Sun

Drei ("three") refers to the restaurant, bar and cocktail lounge sections of this international establishment. The tasty offerings range from Indonesian satay to black coco chicken, and Cape Town ostrich to New Zealand green mussels on lemongrass. **Moderate**

Frannz *cultured German cooking* `4 F1`

Schönhauser Allee 36, Prenzlauer Berg
>> www.frannz.de • 030 72 62 79 36 0
Open from noon Mon -Fri, from 10am Sat & Sun

Attached to a nightclub and popular beer garden *(see p121)*, the always packed Frannz is a meeting place for students, artists and locals. The Wiener schnitzel and fish dishes such as pan-fried pike-perch are sophisticated, yet affordable. **Moderate**

Khushi *authentic Indian cuisine* `4 G1`

Kollwitzstrasse 37, Prenzlauer Berg • 030 41 71 74 23
>> www.khushi-berlin.de
Open noon–midnight Sun–Thu, noon–1am Fri & Sat

"Life is easier if enjoyed" is Khushi's slogan. The extremely long menu includes tandooris and Muglai dishes, and a generous section for vegetarians. The low-priced, high-quality Indian food is relished by a mixed crowd of students and arty types. **Cheap**

>> *Waiters in Berlin tend to be on the gruff side – don't take it personally!*

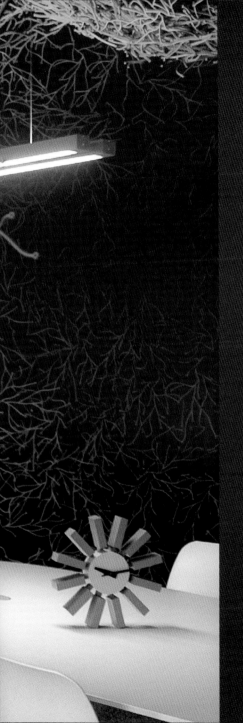

shopping

Shoppers who love fashion and creative design will find that Berlin is their playground. The country's most elegant department stores are here, together with an abundance of quirky boutiques and funky second-hand outlets. Berlin's shops are also strong on antiques, books, art, porcelain and records. And a visit to the city's historic market halls is not to be missed.

SHOPPING

I often think of shopping in Berlin as being like a roller-coaster ride on the cutting edge of Europe's design and fashion scene, swooping from street-level trends to the highs of couture. In a fast-changing shopping scene, it's great fun to hop from one small boutique to the next, searching out all things quirky and cool. No shopping trip should miss out the massive KaDeWe department store, however, nor the delectable foods of Butter-Lindner.

Jürgen Scheunemann

Berlin's Best Emporiums

There is probably no better way to jump-start a shopping spree than a visit to continental Europe's largest department store, **KaDeWe** *(see p63)*. Then head over to **Stilwerk** *(see p61)* to check out the latest furniture and home accessories. For French food, fashions and perfumes, browse the departments of **Galeries Lafayette** *(see p50)*.

Shoes and Hats

For a sophisticated, international look, check out the designer shoes from **Budapester Schuhe** *(see p59)*. If you are searching for something classy but in a hipper vein, try **Adidas Originals Berlin** *(see p55)*. **Fiona Bennett** *(see p51)* is Germany's best milliner, creating fabulous, creative hats for women.

Designer Couture

Berlin has long been a city of avant-garde fashions. You'll find the latest trends and designs at **Berlinomat** *(see p65)*, a funky showcase for some 150 young Berlin designers. **Claudia Skoda Level** *(see p54)* is the high priestess of Berlin's fashion scene, while **Jil Sander** *(see p58)* is the designer of choice for fans of sharp businesswear.

choice shops

Stylish Home Accessories

Head to the **Gipsformerei** *(see p59)* to get a plaster copy of Nefertiti and other antique stars for your living room. If you prefer more racy accessories, the immensely stylish goodies at the **Porsche Design Store** *(see p59)* will be your choice. For a taste of East German nostalgic memorabilia, try **Mondos Art** *(see p64)*.

Gourmet Food

A trip to **Butter-Lindner** *(see p60)* is like visiting a 19th-century grocer's, with fine cheeses, German sausages, salads and freshly baked bread. Equally alluring are **Whisky & Cigars** *(see p51)* – a speciality store crammed with bottles and tobacco – and **Melanie** *(see p62)*, which has a tantalizing selection of chocolates and liqueurs.

Local Colour

For one of Germany's quirkiest stores, pay a visit to **Harry Lehmann** *(see p61)*, an old-fashioned perfume store where you can get your very own mix. An array of Berlin memorabilia is presented by the knowledgeable staff at **Berlin-Story** *(see p51)*, and a selection of vintage and current comics can be found at **Grober Unfug** *(see p64)*.

Galeries Lafayette *French style* `5 C4`
Friedrichstrasse 76–8, Mitte • 030 20 94 80
>> www.galerieslafayette.de Open 10–8 Mon–Sat

Occupying a sleek glass and steel building designed by French architect Jean Nouvel, Galeries Lafayette is a haven for Francophiles. An elegant perfume section, racks of petite clothes and announcements made in a charming French accent set the scene.

This Berlin department store is Lafayette's only major outlet outside France, and remains a fledgling enterprise cherished primarily for its gourmet food section in the basement. Fresh, imported meat pastries, tender Charolais beef cuts, rare goat's cheeses, quince jam from Provence and oysters from Brittany are among the treats. Here, too, you will find the crispiest baguette east of Paris and, of course, a huge selection of wine, including fine Bordeaux and Champagne. Many of the foodstuffs can be eaten at tables or the counters themselves, where steak and fish, salads and cheeses are prepared in front of you.

Fluffy White Pink *candy-coloured fun* `6 F1`
Rosenthaler Strasse 15, Mitte • 030 84 71 29 14
>> www.i-love-kitty.de Open noon–8 Mon–Fri, noon–7 Sat

This is a light-hearted and fun shop for Hello Kitty and other Asian comic character merchandise. The T-shirts and accessories are complemented by moderately priced, one-of-a-kind dresses, skirts and tops, created by small-label Asian designers and appealing to the hip European market.

Neurotitan *art and street culture* `6 F1`
Rosenthaler Strasse 39, Mitte • 030 30 87 25 76
>> www.neurotitan.de Open noon–8 Mon–Sat

Run by the Schwarzenberg artist group, this shop and gallery has long been a meeting point for many of Berlin's most creative minds. Expect to find limited-edition graphic art books, exquisite comics, small-label electronic music on CD and vinyl, silk-screen prints and posters, postcards and badges.

Berlin-Story *all about Berlin*   `5 C3`
Unter den Linden 40, Mitte • 030 20 45 38 42
>> www.berlinstory.de Open 10–7 daily

Not to be confused with the Story of Berlin Museum on Kurfürstendamm, the Berlin-Story shop sells more than 3,000 books about the city (in various languages) and a range of better-than-average souvenirs. There is also a small history exhibition. Best of all, the staff are a mine of information about Berlin.

Hut Up *beautiful woollens for women*   `5 D1`
Oranienburger Strasse 32, Mitte • 030 28 38 61 05
>> www.hutup.de Open 11–7 Mon–Sat

Traditional methods of felting and blocking are used at Hut Up to create a striking range of dresses, blouses, scarves and accessories. The garments – made from the finest merino wool interwoven with silk, linen and cotton – have a timeless elegance that is suitable for business or leisure.

Fiona Bennett *hats for all occasions*   `6 E1`
Grosse Hamburger Strasse 25, Mitte • 030 28 09 63 30
>> www.fionabennett.com
Open 10–6 Mon–Wed, noon–8 Thu & Fri, noon–6 Sat

British designer Fiona Bennett has become Germany's finest milliner. Her creations – mostly playful reinterpretations of classics – are worn by showbiz celebs and the fashion-conscious Mitte girl alike. Her new mini caps are especially versatile.

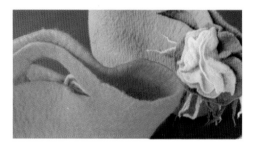

Whisky & Cigars *a hundred whiskies*   `6 E1`
Sophienstrasse 23, Mitte • 030 28 20 37 6
>> www.whisky-cigars.de Open noon–7 Mon–Fri, 11–4 Sat

This charming little store is crammed with shelves of expensive whisky bottles and a walk-in humidor. You can sample before buying the rare Bourbons, Scottish Single Malts and special vintages. Cigars come from Cuba, Honduras, Brazil and Jamaica, ranging from the Montecristo A to the tiny Panetela.

Fishbelly *designer underwear* `6 E1`
Hackesche Höfe, Sophienstrasse 7, Mitte • 030 28 04 51 80
»» www.fishbelly.de Open 12:30–7 Mon–Fri, noon–6 Sat

Located within the exclusive Hackesche Höfe
arcades, this trendy boutique offers an exciting range
of lingerie, running the gamut from sporty to sexy.
Many unusual lines are stocked – the little articles
in fur are among Fishbelly's most popular lines,
especially with the city's large Russian community.

Schön Einrichten *concept-driven interiors* `4 E3`
Joachimstrasse 5, Mitte • 030 28 09 70 11
»» www.schoeneinrichten.de Open noon–7 Tue–Fri, noon–6 Sat

Schön is as much an art gallery as a furniture shop.
International designer names such as E15, Alessi,
Nymphenburg, Modular and WOW provide inspiration
for both home and office. The splendid carpets
and textiles on display come from Shyam Ahuja,
Sakoo Hesslein, Oliver Treutlein and others.

Trippen *shoes to live in* `6 E1`
Hackesche Höfe, Hof 4 & 6, Rosenthaler Strasse 40, Mitte • 030 28 39 13 37
»» www.trippen.com Open 11–8 Mon–Fri (to 7pm in winter), 10–7 Sat

The Trippen flagship store offers all the top collections of the Berlin
shoe manufacturer. A typical shoe here – whether for a man or
woman – will be made from supple elk leather fashioned into a
comfortable, chubby shape with a flat heel. People with wide feet
are spoilt for choice. The women's collection also includes some
classier, strappy designs, with heels in alder wood.

Vintage and Second-Hand Clothing
The hotch-potch chic of so many Berliners is
explained by the city's many second-hand clothing
outlets, which are the haunt of students and
individualists. One of the biggest and cheapest
second-hand shops is **Made in Berlin** (Map 6 F1,
Neue Schönhauser Str. 19, www.kleidermarkt.de),
which can provide the look of anyone from a
1960s hillbilly to 80s new waver or 90s techno
hipster. **Glencheck** (Map 7 B3, Joachim-Friedrich
Str. 34, www.glencheck-berlin.de) offers classic
outfits from the 1920s–50s. **Dawn** (Map 10 F2,
Oranienstrasse 19) focuses on German designer
labels, mainly for women. **Sommerladen** (Map 4 E3,
Linienstrasse 153) stocks pre-worn D&G and Chanel
clothing, among other high-class labels.

Lisa D. *avant-garde fashion for women*   `6 E1`

Hackesche Höfe, Hof 4 & 5, Rosenthaler Strasse 40–41, Mitte
030 28 29 06 1
>> www.lisad.com Open 11–7 Mon–Sat, noon–4 Sun

The creative lines – named Sweet and Low, Either Or and suchlike – include smart clothes and flamboyant outfits for the most extravagant parties. There are two outlets in the Hackesche Höfe – head for courtyard 5 for last season's fashion at a discount.

Wunderkind Boutique *the real Joop*   `4 E3`

Rückerstrasse 8, Mitte • 030 28 04 05 85
>> www.wunderkind.de Open 11–8 Mon–Fri, 10–6 Sat

Top designer Wolfgang Joop's Wunderkind label is a far cry from the mass-produced Joop clothing available at department stores. The swinging, black or earth-coloured dresses are a hit with nonchalant, worldly women, and his range of bodycare products will help any stressed-out lady to get her glow back.

RSVP *products for your desktop*   `4 E3`

Mulackstrasse 14, Mitte • 030 28 09 46 44
>> www.rsvp-berlin.de Open noon–7 Mon–Fri, noon–4 Sat

This paper and stationery shop, founded by a graphic designer, is a place where craftsmanship is still valued. Here you will find the complete Moleskine collection of notebooks, along with Japanese ink-stones, California Clipiola paperclips and Florentine calfskin cases for business cards.

Hundt Hammer Stein *literary oasis*   `4 F3`

Alte Schönhauser Str. 23–4, Mitte • 030 23 45 76 69
>> www.hundthammerstein.de

Open 11–7:30 Mon–Fri, 11–7 Sat

Two friendly and knowledgeable literary buffs run this basement bookshop. The well-sorted stock includes biographies, children's books, travel guides and poetry, and is especially strong on English-language books, gay literature and books about Berlin.

Claudia Skoda Level *designer knitwear* `4 F3`

Alte Schönhauser Strasse 35, Mitte • 030 28 07 21 1
>> www.claudiaskoda.com Open noon–8 Mon–Fri, noon–7 Sat

For decades, Claudia Skoda has helped to maintain Berlin's status as Germany's avant-garde fashion city, and surprisingly she still stays ahead of the much younger designer crowd. It has been said that Skoda's collections – which rely heavily on colourful knitted dresses and knitted accessories such as gloves, cuffs and hats – come closer than any other German fashion house to defining the Berlin style.

   Most designs follow classic, no-nonsense forms. Some dress cuts (playfully named Wildflower, My Pearl and so on) are reminiscent of the chaste dresses of the 1950s. However, the collections also feature more urban, upbeat designs for both men and women, intriguing retro styles, futuristic shiny colours and non-knitted, suave materials. A new line, called Clask, is the most affordable range, while an expensive custom-tailored service is also available.

Smart Travelling *travellers' essentials* `4 F3`

Münzstrasse 21, Mitte • 030 28 09 36 99
>> www.smart-travelling.com
Open noon–7:30 Mon–Fri, noon–6 Sat

This unusual travel agent is a useful combination of Internet-booking facility, shop and travellers' club, offering clients travel programmes to around 20 European cities. The shop stocks bags, travel kits, cosmetics and rare souvenirs from the various cities.

CD and Record Shops

Berlin's rich music scene is reflected in the shops selling recorded music. The four-storey **Kulturkauf-haus Dussmann** (Map 5 C3, Friedrichstr. 90, www.kulturkaufhaus.de) has a huge classical department and stocks the latest rock, pop and dance CDs. **L&P Classics** (Map 8 E1, Knesebeckstr. 33–4) specializes in classical music. Smaller shops include **Vopo Records** (Map 4 F1, Danziger Str. 31, www.vopo-records.de), which is great for punk and hardcore, and budget outlets such as **Apollo Disc** (Map 7 D1, Kantstr. 52, www.apollo-disc.de). Kitschy **Platten Pedro** (Map 1 B3, Tegeler Weg 102, www.platten-pedro.de) is devoted to secondhand vinyl. **Space Hall** (Map 9 D4, Zossener Str. 13, www.space-hall.de) is good for both vinyl and CDs.

Andreas Murkudis *idiosyncratic trio* `4 F3`
Münzstrasse 21 (second yard), Mitte • 030 30 88 19 45
Open noon–8 Mon–Fri, noon–6 Sat

In an ordinary Berlin backyard, Andreas Murkudis, the former director of Museum der Dinge (a museum of mundane objects and furniture), has come up with a unique retail concept based on his own eclectic tastes in clothing, accessories and furniture. The result is three highly contrasting shops.

In the first shop you will find travel accessories, Schiesser underwear, Berlin-made Hamann chocolates and Eau de Berlin perfumes. The second shop sells women's fashion labels, including Martine Margiela, Yamamoto and Kostas Murkudis (the owner's brother), Felisi leather goods and jewellery from young Berlin designers. The third shop mixes menswear with design accessories and furniture. Alongside the Stich shirts you will find an ever-changing display of furniture from Vogt + Weizenegger and Mooi, and a line of bespoke bedclothes from Haltbar.

Adidas Originals Berlin *cult classics* `4 F3`
Münzstrasse 13–15, Mitte • 030 27 59 43 81
» www.adidas.com Open 11–8 Mon–Sat

German footwear giant Adidas, the strongest global competitor to Nike, has always been a cult in Germany. Even 30 years ago, there was a social stigma for any kid who could not tie up a three-stripes – only a two-stripes, no-name sneaker – in the locker room. Retro Adidas sports shoes are collectors' items and rank among the hippest streetwear, certainly in Mitte.

The classic retro Adidas footwear comes in bright colours that hark back to the pop art of the 1960s and 70s. The store sells newly developed retro collections like the Respect Me! line, designed in collaboration with US singer Missy Elliot. For those who are more interested in the practical use than retro rating of the products, there are plainer-coloured shoes and clothing for running, basketball, tennis and other sports. The once mocked but now popular Adilette shower room sandal is available, too.

Breathe *fresh cosmetics* `6 F2`

Rochstrasse 17, Mitte • 030 24 34 25 77
>> www.breathe-cosmetics.com
Open noon–8 Mon–Fri, noon–6 Sat

Breathe's elegant store was created by up-and-coming architects Room Safari. Inside, high-quality cosmetic brands such as Julisis, Sphatika and Hamadi sit next to extravagant perfumes and hair products from Alchera, Monyette, 06130 and Sissel Tolaas.

Blush *apparel for the boudoir* `6 G1`

Rosa-Luxemburg-Strasse 22, Mitte • 030 28 09 35 80
>> www.blush-berlin.com
Open noon–8 Mon–Fri, noon–7 Sat

Berlin's prettiest lingerie shop has the feel of a 1950s boutique, complete with an atelier in which Blush's own line is made. Other brands are just as exclusive and sexy: Fifi Chachnil, Mey Blumarine, Maliza, Princesse Tam Tam and Revenge De La Femme.

Belleville *international cutting-edge design* `6 G1`

Rosa-Luxemburg-Strasse 27, Mitte • 030 24 62 83 71
>> www.belleville-store.de Open noon–8 Mon–Sat

The Belleville shop is part of a multimedia project linked with a contemporary art gallery, called Belle Views, and design magazine *Bell*. Young fashion designers such as Misericordia (Peru), Medinastar (Morocco), Nudie Jeans (Sweden) and Airbag (Germany) contribute to the seasonal collections.

Apartment *urban outfitters* `6 G1`

Memhardstrasse 8, Mitte • 030 28 04 22 53
>> www.apartmentberlin.de Open noon–8 Mon–Fri, noon–6 Sat

Racks and racks of designer clothing include Apartment's own-label T-shirts and bags. The hip urban look conveyed by Marc Jacobs, Chicks on Speed, Bernhard Wilhelm and others is perfect for Berlin's nightclubs, while shoes by N.D.C. or Visvim Deerskin offer both street-cred and comfort.

Jil Sander *sharp style for women* `7 D2`

Kurfürstendamm 185, Charlottenburg • 030 88 67 02 0
>> www.jilsander.com Open 10–7 Mon–Fri, 10–6 Sat

The clear-cut, almost puritanical clothes by high-profile German designer Jil Sander (who made the little black dress fashionable in Germany) are a great alternative to Prada, Gucci and Chanel. Her soft-falling, exquisite materials, mostly in black and sand colours, can be worn for business and after work.

Porsche Design Store *covetable objects* `7 D2`
Kurfürstendamm 190–92, Charlottenburg • 030 88 71 78 3
»» www.porsche-design.de Open 10–7 Mon–Fri, 10–6 Sat

It doesn't necessarily have to be a Porsche Boxster or 911. The Porsche engineers have combined perfect German technology with timeless style to create a range of pens, watches, clasp knives, sunglasses and other accessories. The radio-controlled toy Porsches might satisfy those who can't afford the real thing.

Manufactum *quality products, quality food* `8 E1`
Hardenbergstrasse 4–5, Charlottenburg • 030 24 03 38 44
»» www.manufactum.de Open 10–8 Mon–Fri, 10–6 Sat

A modern day general store, Manufactum stocks well-selected, finely crafted house and garden items, stylish but no-nonsense office supplies, and natural cosmetics. In the adjoining food section, Brot & Butter, you can watch your bread and pastries being baked while sipping an espresso at the bar.

Budapester Schuhe *classy footwear* `8 E2`
Kurfürstendamm 199, Charlottenburg • 030 88 62 42 06
»» www.budapester-schuhe.de Open 10–7 Mon–Fri, 10–6 Sat

Handmade Budapester and Oxford shoes by Laszlo Vass are the classics, joined these days by Tod's, Gucci and Chanel for both men and women. Staff at the city's most elegant shoe store zealously guard the treasures. (Lower prices and friendlier salespeople can be found in an outlet at Bleibtreustrasse 24.)

Gipsformerei *Nefertiti to go* `1 A5`
Sophie-Charlotten-Str. 17–18, Charlottenburg • 030 32 67 69 0
Open 9–4 Mon, Tue, Thu & Fri, 9–6 Wed

For more than 150 years the Gipsformerei (Replica Workshop) has been reproducing classical busts for Germany's state museums and clients around the world. On sale to the public are plaster models of Queen Nefertiti, seals and other icons from the ancient world – fantastic for the house or garden.

Patrick Hellmann metro look for men `7 D2`
Bleibtreustrasse 36, Charlottenburg • 030 88 26 96 1
>> www.patrickhellmann.com
Open 9:30–7 Mon & Tue, 9:30–8 Wed–Fri, 9:30–6 Sat

Of his seven formal menswear stores in the city, this is Hellmann's biggest and most classy. The elegant clothing is handmade and includes many English-influenced pin-striped suits made from the best grade of wool and cut with Italian-style flair.

Butter-Lindner old-fashioned delicatessen `8 E1`
Knesebeckstrasse 92, Charlottenburg • 030 31 35 37 5
>> www.butter-lindner.de
Open 8–6 Mon–Fri, 8–1:30 Sat

Originally a butter shop, Butter-Lindner has grown into a chain of delis, selling the finest cheeses, sausages, salads, breads and hot foods. This outlet is a typical neighbourhood store, with old-fashioned counters and starched-aproned sales assistants.

Bücherbogen coffee-table books `8 E1`
Savignyplatz, S-Bahnbogen 593, Charlottenburg • 030 31 21 93 2
>> www.buecherbogen.com Open 10–8 Mon–Fri, 10–6 Sat

Set within arches under the railway tracks, this art bookshop has an inviting, intellectual vibe. Beautiful volumes on art, architecture, photography and film are stacked up to the curved ceiling, and tremble whenever a train passes. The staff are knowledgeable about the rarest art books, new and old.

Snea-q sneakers for ardent fans `8 E1`
Fasanenstrasse 81, Charlottenburg • 030 31 99 69 62
>> www.snea-q.de Open 11–8 Mon–Fri, 10–8 Sat

This new store is the high temple for sports shoes fetishists, who will find the latest, hippest collectables for the feet here. Displaying its wares like works of art, Snea-q focuses on rare models, both European and American, from makers such as Adidas, Asics, Diadora, DKNY, Onitsuka Tiger and Y-3.

Stilwerk *stylish furniture complex* `8 E1`

Kantstrasse 17, Charlottenburg • 030 31 51 50
» www.stilwerk.de
Open 10–8 Mon–Fri, 10–6 Sat, 2–6 Sun (viewing only on Sun)

A high-tech building with 20,000 sq m (215,000 sq ft) of floor space, Berlin's fashionable Stilwerk complex is a world of soothing interior design. This is not strictly a department store, but more a group of showrooms, which – true to Stilwerk's maxim that "cooperation beats competition" – brings many of Europe's top design companies under one roof.

Products by Alessi, B+B Italia, Cassina, Gaggenau, Kartell, Ligne Roset and others cater to the current vogue for minimalist, curvy furniture, multiple spot-lighting and ergonomic kitchen implements. The Bang & Olufsen outlet displays its stylish range of audio and video equipment, and there's also a Bechstein piano showroom. Even by German standards, the prices here are steep, but there's usually a sale to be found somewhere on the four floors.

Harry Lehmann *the scents of Berlin* `8 E1`

Kantstrasse 106, Charlottenburg • 030 32 43 58 2
Open 9–6:30 Mon–Fri, 9–2 Sat

Since 1926, this riotous shop has specialized in perfumes. Not the limited range sold in every airport and department store around the world, but hand-made, mainly floral distillations for men and women – literally hundreds of fragrances, presented in lovely flacons and phials, and at great prices.

Dopo Domani *contemporary interiors* `8 E1`

Kantstrasse 148, Charlottenburg • 030 88 22 24 2
» www.dopo-domani.com Open 10:30–7 Mon–Fri, 10–6 Sat

One of the more ambitious interior design showrooms in upmarket Charlottenburg, Dopo Domani caters mainly to clients wanting tailor-made makeovers (rather than off-the-peg solutions) for their homes. Names such as Porro, Minotti, Flex Form and Capellini provide the furnishings over three floors.

Melanie *confectionery and more* `8 E1`
Goethestrasse 4, Charlottenburg • 030 31 38 33 0
Open 10–7 Mon, Tue, Wed & Fri, 10–2 Sat

Herr Präller sells almost 100 varieties of handmade truffles and bars of chocolate alongside 4,000 other gourmet foods, including teas, spices, jams and liqueurs from the finest international purveyors. His enticing shop is also known as Paradis Nebenstelle ("branch office of Paradise").

Schuhtick *footwear mainly for women* `8 F2`
Tauentzienstrasse 5, Charlottenburg • 030 21 40 98 0
Also at Savignyplatz 11 & Potsdamer Platz Arkaden
>> www.schuhtick.de Open 10–8 Mon–Sat

The Schuhtick stores are known for their trendy yet well-made shoes, usually priced under 120 euros. Men have a very limited selection, but women are well catered for with a vast range of pumps, high-heels, clogs, sneakers, boots and sandals.

Hugendubel *paradise for bookworms* `8 F2`
Tauentzienstrasse 13, Charlottenburg • 01801 48 44 84
>> www.hugendubel.de Open 9:30–8 Mon–Sat

This four-storey outlet of Germany's biggest bookstore chain is an ocean of packed shelves surrounding quiet islands of lounge-like reading areas. German and foreign-language books, comics, games and videos are stocked. On the ground floor is a bargain area; on the first floor is a café for coffee and cakes.

Market Halls and Specialist Markets
Berlin has long been a paradise for bargain-hunters. The biggest and best antiques and art market is the **Strasse des 17. Juni Markt** (Map 2 G5, Sat & Sun), where professional dealers operate. With persistence and know-how, you should be able to strike a fair deal here. Food markets abound, such as the lovely quaint one at **Karl-August-Platz** in Charlottenburg (Map 7 D1, Sat) and the market at **Wittenbergplatz** in Schöneberg (Map 8 G2, Sat). Equally enticing are the two old *Markthalle* (market halls) at **Marheineke** in Kreuzberg (Map 9 D4) and **Arminius** in Tiergarten (Map 2 F3, both Mon–Sat). Another must is a visit to the **Türkischer Markt** on Maybachufer (Map 10 G3, Tue & Fri), which offers a feast of Middle Eastern scents and tastes.

KaDeWe *international emporium*   `8 G2`

Tauentzienstrasse 21–4, Schöneberg • 030 21 21 0
» www.kadewe.de Open 10–8 Mon–Fri, 9:30–8 Sat

What Bloomingdale's is to New York, Harrods to London and Lafayette to Paris, KaDeWe is to Berlin. One of the city's main landmarks, this 60,000 sq m (nearly 650,000 sq ft) colossus off Wittenbergplatz is a department store selling every imaginable product.

Founded in 1907, Kaufhaus des Westens ("Department Store of the West") was the fancy department store for the nouveaux riches of this new part of Berlin (hence the name, which has nothing to do with the West Berlin of the Cold War). The store was destroyed in World War II, then rebuilt to its original glamour in the 1950s, becoming the symbol of the West German postwar economic upswing, right in the face of the Socialist bloc. It has been extended several times since. The most celebrated features of the seven-storey building are its two soaring atriums and glass elevators that glide up and down. The flagship of the Karstadt-Quelle retail empire has also undergone a further expensive makeover in honour of its 100th anniversary.

Top designer brands are represented by their own stylish shops on the ground level, and there is a vast range of international designer clothing for men and women on the floors above. KaDeWe's sixth floor is legendary – a gourmet's paradise with more than 33,000 foodstuffs, including 1,300 cheeses, 400 different breads, 1,200 types of sausages, and about 2,400 international wines. Best of all are the Paul Bocuse counter for French country cooking, the sushi bar for fresh fish and the adjacent seafood barbecue counter. On Fridays and Saturdays, this floor is the haunt of local celebrities and Germany's wealthy elite: just as it was 100 years ago.

Grober Unfug *devoted to comics* `9 D3`

Zossener Strasse 32–3, Kreuzberg • 030 69 40 14 90
»» www.groberunfug.de Open 11–7 Mon–Fri, 11–4 Sat

This crowded store is arguably the best comic shop in Germany. Stacked in yellow plastic boxes are hundreds of vintage and current comics for both children and adults, including foreign editions of all major titles and many Japanese Manga volumes. The rarest titles are displayed behind glass.

Die Imaginäre Manufaktur (DIM) `10 G2`

Oranienstrasse 26, Kreuzberg • 030 28 50 30 0
»» www.blindenanstalt.de Open 10–7 Mon–Fri, 10–2 Sat

DIM is a workshop founded by blind craftspeople, which sells everyday household products, such as brooms, brushes, furniture and wickerwork. The workshop has a long history – blind people have worked here for about 130 years, for most of the time making and selling traditional brooms and brushes.

In 1998 the industrial designers Oliver Vogt and Hermann Weizenegger enlisted the help of these highly skilled craftspeople to develop a contemporary line of products, including lamps, key rings, chairs and even shoes. Some of the products – which are well made and sometimes slightly quirky looking – are displayed in galleries and sold around the world. In 2005 the workshop was taken over from the Blind Institute by a private group, but blind people are still involved in making the products, and every euro spent here still goes in direct support of the blind.

Mondos Art *souvenirs from East Berlin* `11 C1`

Schreinerstrasse 6, Friedrichshain • 030 42 01 07 78
»» www.mondosarts.de Open 10–7 Mon–Fri, 11–4 Sat

East German and Socialist memorabilia is the theme here. Among the items ranging from kitsch to groovy, you might find something worth taking home, such as a T-shirt with the cheerful *Ampelmännchen* from the traffic lights in East Berlin *(see p31)* or the (ideology-free) *Sandman* animations for children.

Berlinomat *contemporary Berlin design* 11 D1

Frankfurter Allee 89, Friedrichshain • 030 42 08 14 45
>> www.berlinomat.com Open 11–8 Mon–Fri, 10–6 Sat ✓

This funky, alternative fashion store sells cutting-edge designs for the young urban generation. About 150 Berlin-based designers present an exciting range of jewellery, furniture, homewares and clothing. The styles are as mixed as the city, but one common inspiration seems to be snippets of 1950s or 60s graphics and styling. Here is the fashion you will probably be seeing on MTV a year from now.

All items at Berlinomat are unique designer pieces and yet surprisingly affordable. The racks include revival fashions such as Zeha, the East German sneakers. Some of the most fashionable (and thus increasingly valuable) pieces include those by Hasipop, Ic!berlin, Dreigold, RMX and Formfalt.

Lately, the avant-garde has started to be absorbed by the mainstream: Galeries Lafayette *(see p50)* now carries selected Berlinomat items.

Luxus International *artists' laboratory* 4 F1

Kastanienallee 101, Prenzlauer Berg • 030 44 32 48 77
>> www.luxus-international.de Open noon–8 Mon–Sat ✓

The Luxus project has garnered much attention since it was opened in 2002 by firebrand entrepreneur Sebastian Mücke. The concept store is located in the middle of Prenzlauer Berg (an East Berlin district whose population of young and aspiring artists, designers and media types seems to grow by the day) and it epitomizes the heterogeneous nature of Berlin's contemporary design scene. The idea is that artists, artisans and designers, for a monthly fee, can put almost anything up for sale in the store. Some 250 creators use Luxus as a platform to try out their products and experiments with potential buyers.

Not everything at Luxus is fantastic, but the sheer creativity of products on display can be both awe-inspiring and hilarious. Shop here for your next Astro-turf necklace, recycled plastic handbag, felt elephant or jewellery made from computer components.

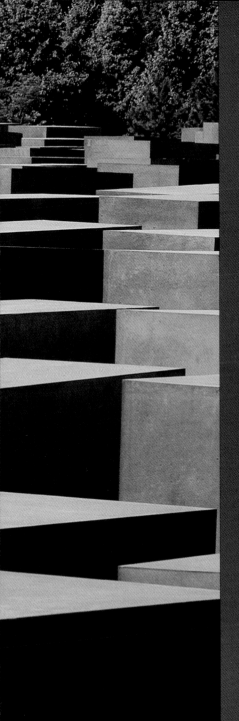

art &
architecture

Berlin's turbulent history is reflected in its architecture, which ranges from restored Prussian mansions to post-Wall showpieces by internationally acclaimed architects. Avant-garde movements such as Dada and the Bauhaus school found a home in this city in the early 20th century, and Berlin continues to be a hotbed of creativity. Local artists are well represented in the city's world-class art galleries and museums.

ART & ARCHITECTURE

Consolidating the cultural life of what was once a divided city has proved fruitful, and many of Berlin's world-class collections are now displayed in stunning new homes, while exisiting architectural masterpieces have been restored to their full glory. Berlin has long been a magnet for artists, and since reunification the city has boomed with creative activity. Many important contemporary art galleries have settled in Berlin, bringing with them clients, more artists, and exhibitions galore.

Constance Hanna

A Once-Divided City

Get a glimpse into Berlin's historic role in Europe's Cold War face-off at the reconstructed border crossing, **Checkpoint Charlie** *(see p14)*. The workings of the East German secret police are revealed at the **Stasi Museum** *(see p83)*, while the longest remaining section of the Berlin Wall is now a **"gallery"** *(see p130)* of international art.

Landmarks

Berlin's **Fernsehturm** *(see p72)* is visible from all the city's central districts and is useful for getting your bearings, as is the striking design of Scharoun's **Staatsbibliothek** *(see p75)*. On the Kurfürstendamm, the rebuilding of this city by combining the war-torn with the modern is epitomized by the **Kaiser-Wilhelm-Gedächtnis-Kirche** *(see p79)*.

Jewish Berlin

Follow 2,000 years of German-Jewish history at the groundbreaking **Jüdisches Museum** *(see p82)*. Post-reunification restoration of the **Neue Synagoge** *(see p73)* is a reminder of the city's heritage while pointing to Berlin's Jewish renaissance. And the **Holocaust Denkmal** *(see p75)* is designed to symbolize the fate of Jews in Nazi Germany.

choice sights

Major Art Collections

Among Berlin's most outstanding world-class collections of European art are the 13th–18th century paintings at the **Gemäldegaleric** *(see p78)*, 19th-century German masters of sculpture and painting at the rebuilt **Alte Nationalgalerie** *(see p71)*, and 20th-century modern greats from Picasso to Richter at the **Neue Nationalgalerie** *(see p77)*.

Modern Art

The **Hamburger Bahnhof** *(see p74)* displays modern masters, including Beuys and Warhol, and more recent artists such as Kippenberger, Polke and Nauman. **Kunst-Werke Berlin** *(see p73)* showcases the stars of the current scene, and the **Berlinische Galerie** *(see p73)* hosts contemporary exhibitions and retrospectives of 20th-century art movements.

Historical Museums

For an in-depth look at German history, go to the newly reopened **Deutsches Historisches Museum** *(see p70)*. The world-renowned **Pergamonmuseum** *(see p70)* contains treasures from ancient Greece, Rome and the Near East, while **Schloss Charlottenburg** *(see p80)* offers a glimpse into the opulent world of Germany's past nobility.

Deutsches Historisches Museum `6 E3`
Unter den Linden 2, Mitte • 030 20 30 40
>> www.dhm.de Open 10–6 daily

Dedicated to the history of Germany, this vast museum is packed with works of art, militaria and objects from everyday life. About half the collection covers the first centuries AD up to 1918; the rest dates from the Weimar Republic, the Nazi regime and the postwar period up to the mid-1990s. Topics include the relationship between men and women through the ages, and the changing patterns of work.

The permanent collection is housed in the Baroque Zeughaus, which was built in 1706 as an armoury of the Prussian military. After renovation, the museum reopened in May 2006, with a new wing designed by the US architect I M Pei. An underground passage connects the Zeughaus to Pei's wing, which is a light and airy palace of white marble designed to house temporary exhibitions on subjects relating to German social history. **Adm** (free on Mon)

Pergamonmuseum *classical antiquities* `5 D2`
Bodestr. 1–3 (entrance on Kupfergraben), Mitte • 030 20 90 55 77
>> www.smb.spk-berlin.de Open 10–6 Tue–Sun (to 10pm Thu)

Located on an island in the Spree (the Museumsinsel), the Pergamon boasts an outstanding collection of archeological treasures from ancient Greece and Rome, and the ancient Near East. It is one of the best museums of its kind in the world, with the crowds to prove it. Arrive early to avoid the worst of the melee.

The museum's highlight is the imposing, restored Pergamon Altar, dating from the 2nd century BC, which fills the main hall. This is encircled by a magnificent reconstructed frieze depicting *The Battle of the Giants and the Gods*, also from Pergamon (in modern-day Turkey). Other impressive exhibits include the colourful 6th-century BC Babylonian Ishtar Gate and Processional Way in the Ancient Near East collection. The opposite wing contains Hellenistic and Roman sculpture, jewellery and coins, and on the upper level is the famous Museum of Islamic Art. **Adm**

Alte Nationalgalerie German masters   6 E2

Bodestrasse 1–3, Mitte • 030 20 90 58 01
>> www.smb.spk-berlin.de   Open 10–6 Tue–Sun (to 10pm Thu)

Also located on the Museumsinsel, the Alte Nationalgalerie contains an incomparable collection of 19th-century German paintings and sculptures, which are housed in a Neo-Classical building designed by Friedrich August Stüler in the 1870s. Extensive renovation was undertaken after World War II and again after the reunification of Germany. The current airy galleries opened in 2001.

From the beginning, the Nationalgalerie was dedicated to promoting the German nation through the arts. Today, however, this old (Alte) branch also houses some important French Impressionist works, while the new (Neue) Nationalgalerie (see p77) houses an international collection of modern art.

The Alte Nationalgalerie is arranged chronologically, beginning on the top floor. The larger room on this floor contains landscape paintings executed with technical virtuosity by the famous Berlin architect Carl Friedrich Schinkel (1781–1841). Beyond this is a room devoted to Caspar David Friedrich (1774–1840), the most exalted German Romantic painter. The works include his highly atmospheric Monk by the Sea and Abbey in the Oakwoods, both of which brought him adulation when first exhibited in 1810.

The middle floor is given over to temporary shows, as well as a permanent collection of paintings by German Symbolists and French Impressionists: The Isle of the Dead (1883) by Arnold Böcklin and Edouard Manet's In the Winter Garden (1879) are among the highlights. An entire wing on the ground floor is dedicated to the Realist painter Adolf von Menzel (1815–1905), who captured minute detail and difficult lighting conditions in paintings such as The Iron Rolling Mill and the more intimate Balcony Room. Audio tours, available in several languages, are included in the ticket price. For snacks, seek out the tiny espresso bar inside the gift shop. **Adm**

>> The Museumsinsel is a complex of museums located at the tip of an island in the Spree (see p12)

Art & Architecture

Berliner Dom *august cathedral* `6 E3`
Am Lustgarten 1, Mitte • 030 20 26 91 28
>> www.berliner-dom.de
Open Apr–Sep: 9–8 daily; Oct–Mar: 9–7 daily

The current *Dom*, or Cathedral, dates from 1905, a Wilhelmine, Neo-Baroque structure built to replace an 18th-century Neo-Classical church, which itself had been built on the site of an older church. The main sanctuary is typical of the bombastic Wilhelmine period, with ornate decorations, ceiling mosaics and beautiful altar windows. Statues of eminent 16th-century Lutherans such as Melanchthon, Zwingli and Martin Luther himself add to the grandeur.

For a superb view of central Berlin, weather permitting, climb the 267 steps up to the dome itself. Also worth viewing is the 15th-century crypt, where the rulers of Prussia lie in tombs ranging from simple wooden boxes to ornate sarcophagi, alongside many tiny coffins of infants. Church services on Sundays at 10am are interpreted into English for visitors. **Adm**

Fernsehturm (TV Tower) `6 G2`
Panoramastrasse 1A, Mitte • 030 24 23 33 3
>> www.berlinerfernsehturm.de
Open 9am–midnight daily (from 10am Nov–Feb)

On a clear day, it is worth the wait to be whisked up by elevator to the circular observation deck and slowly rotating café of this landmark 1960s tower. The huge, angled windows, some 204 m (669 ft) above the city, offer spectacular views. **Adm**

Sammlung Hoffmann *private collection* `6 E1`
Sophienstrasse 21, Mitte • 030 28 49 91 21
>> www.sophie-gips.de Open 11–4 Sat (by appointment only)

Make an appointment for a 90-minute tour in English or German (specify when you call) of Erika Hoffmann's private contemporary art collection. The displays are changed annually, and you might see works by Lucio Fontana or Douglas Gordon. Afterwards, try the freshly baked pie at Barcomi's, in the courtyard. **Adm**

Neue Synagoge *rebuilt synagogue* `5 D1`
Oranienburger Strasse 28–30, Mitte • 030 88 02 84 51
>> www.cjudaicum.de Open 10–6 Sun–Thu (to 8pm Sun &
Mon in summer), 10–2 Fri (to 5pm in summer)

The Neue Synagoge's gold-filigreed, Moorish-style
dome can be seen from afar, and when completed
in 1866 it was the source of considerable pride for
Berlin's Jewish community. Designed by Eduard
Knoblauch and inspired in part by the Alhambra in
Spain, the 3,200-seat synagogue was the largest in
Germany, with the top of its dome some 50 m (160 ft)
in height. The synagogue was only slightly damaged
during the Kristallnacht of 1938, when Jewish
buildings were attacked, but in 1945 it was wrecked
by Allied bombing. Now deconsecrated, the rebuilt
structure serves as a museum, with a permanent
display about the building's past, and temporary
exhibitions about Jewish life. There are regular tours
in German (2pm & 4pm Sun, 4pm Wed); English-
language tours can be booked in advance. **Adm**

Kunst-Werke Berlin *influential art space* `5 D1`
Auguststrasse 69, Mitte • 030 24 34 59 0
>> www.kw-berlin.de Open noon–7 Tue–Sun (to 9 Thu)

This former margarine factory was transformed in the
1990s into the city's most influential contemporary art
space. Exhibitions in the hall present established
stars and emerging talent. The huge glass cube in the
courtyard is a café designed by conceptual artist Dan
Graham – a good place for people-watching. **Adm**

Contemporary Art Galleries
Mitte's Scheunenviertel quarter *(see p125)* is home
to many top galleries, including **Wohnmaschine**
for cutting-edge art (Map 5 D1, Tucholskystr. 35,
www.wohnmaschine.de); **C/O** for photography
(Map 5 C1, Linienstr. 144, www.co-berlin.com);
and **Eigen + Art** for rising artists (Map 5 D1,
Auguststr. 26, www.eigen-art.com).

Elsewhere in Mitte, the **Deutsche Guggenheim**
(Map 5 D3, www.deutsche-bank-kunst.com/
guggenheim) puts on shows that change every few
months, many of them specially commissioned.
In Kreuzberg, the **Berlinische Galerie** (Map 10 E2,
Alte Jakobstr. 124–8, www.berlinischegalerie.de)
opened in 2004 and shows modern and contemporary art and photography with a Berlin theme.

Hamburger Bahnhof *art behemoth* **3 B3**

Invalidenstrasse 50–51, Tiergarten • 030 39 78 34 11
➤➤ www.hamburgerbahnhof.de
Open 10–6 Tue–Fri, 11–8 Sat, 11–6 Sun

Set in a handsomely redesigned train station dating from the mid-19th century, the Hamburger Bahnhof is an offshoot of the Neue Nationalgalerie *(see p77)* and showcases several private collections of modern and contemporary art. The main hall and wings house the exceptional Erich Marx collection, which includes famous works by North American and German artists.

The entire west wing is devoted to Joseph Beuys (1921–86) and includes seminal installations such as the strewn stone slabs of *The End of the Twentieth Century*, as well as hundreds of works on paper.

In the main hall are absorbing large-scale paintings and sculptures by Beuys's German student Anselm Kiefer, including the leaden aeroplane of *Mohn und Gedächtnis* ("Poppies and Remembrance") and the oversize books in his *Volkszählung* ("Census").

The adjoining east wing is dominated by Andy Warhol's modern icons, such as one of his vast portraits of Mao and his notorious Disaster Series, which includes *Big Electric Chair*. Warhol's engaging pre-pop drawings are occasionally on display. Offering an Expressionistic contrast to Warhol are a number of Cy Twombly paintings and collages by Robert Rauschenberg.

A recent addition to the Hamburger Bahnhof is the Friedrich Christian Flick collection, which is housed in the 300-m (1,000-ft) long Rieck Halls. This is one of the world's largest and most important collections of modern art. It includes 20th-century pieces by Marcel Duchamp and strong photography, video and multimedia works. German and international stars represented in the collection include Martin Kippenberger, Bruce Nauman, Sigmar Polke and Nam June Paik. Stop for a coffee in the espresso bar when you need a breather, or head to the upmarket café in the main building. **Adm**

Holocaust Denkmal *remembrance* `5 A4`
Cora-Berliner-Strasse 1, Mitte • 030 20 07 66 0
>> www.holocaust-mahnmal.de • Denkmal open 24 hours
daily; information centre open 10–8 Tue–Sun

Opened in 2005, the Holocaust Denkmal, also known
as the Holocaust Mahnmal ("memorial and warning
from the past"), is an extraordinary work of art,
composed of thousands of grey concrete slabs set out
in a vast grid. Visitors can walk in single file among
the stelae, which differ slightly in height to create an
undulating landscape. It was created by the New York
architect Peter Eisenman, who describes the context
of the memorial as "the enormity of the banal".

Below ground is an information centre with
an exhibition about the Holocaust. There are
testimonies from survivors along with a database
for researching the names of those who died. Security
is high – allow a wait of 20 minutes to an hour to
access the halls. (Access to the stelae is open.)
The site is not recommended for children under 14.

Haus der Kulturen der Welt `3 A4`
John-Foster-Dulles-Allee 10, Tiergarten • 030 39 78 71 75
>> www.hkw.de Open 10–9 Tue–Sun

Located in the spectacular former congress hall
(nicknamed the "pregnant oyster"), the House of
World Cultures puts on world music concerts, world
cinema and exhibitions about other cultures. The
Multikulti radio station is also based here *(see p93)*,
as are various festivals *(see pp18–19)*. **Adm**

Staatsbibliothek *landmark building* `9 B1`
Potsdamer Strasse 33, Tiergarten • 030 26 60
>> www.staatsbibliothek-berlin.de
Open 9–9 Mon–Fri, 9–7 Sat

This late-Modernist landmark was designed by Hans
Scharoun and Edgar Wisniewski in the 1960s. Its high
ceilings and mix of natural and artificial light give it
the quasi-sacral atmosphere that attracted Wim
Wenders to film scenes for *Wings of Desire* here.

Kunstgewerbemuseum *decorative arts* `9 A1`
Tiergartenstrasse 6, Tiergarten • 030 26 62 90 2
>> www.smb.spk-berlin.de Open 10–6 Tue–Fri, 11–6 Sat & Sun

Although there is a chronological order to this
museum, from the Middle Ages to the present, it is
more fun simply to meander through the rich collection
of decorative arts. The famous Guelf dynasty treasure
(Welfenschatz) of religious relics is unforgettable, as
are the fabulous cabinets of curiosities. **Adm**

Art & Architecture

Kupferstichkabinett *prints & drawings* `9 A1`
Matthäikirchplatz 8, Tiergarten • 030 26 62 00 2
>> www.kupferstichkabinett.de
Open 10–6 Tue–Fri, 11–6 Sat & Sun

This enormous world-class collection of drawings and prints encompasses a wide cross-section of Western art, from the Middle Ages to the present. But its special emphasis is on iconic artists of the 20th century, such as Picasso, Beckmann, Giacometti and Beuys. **Adm**

Filmmuseum Berlin *celluloid history* `9 B1`
Potsdamer Strasse 2 (Sony Center), Tiergarten • 030 30 09 03 0
>> www.filmmuseum-berlin.de
Open 10–6 Tue–Sun (to 8pm Thu)

The film museum has two areas of focus: German cinema and special effects. Old tricks of the trade are revealed through models used in films such as *King Kong*. The Marlene Dietrich collection includes photos, costumes, documents and letters. **Adm**

Bauhaus-Archiv *museum of design* `8 H1`
Klingelhöferstrasse 14, Tiergarten • 030 25 40 02 78 (infoline)
>> www.bauhaus.de Open 10–5 Wed–Mon

Set back from the street in an oasis of green, Walter Gropius's intriguing building houses a permanent exhibition that offers a concise and unpretentious introduction to the ideology and practice of the Bauhaus – the 20th-century's most important school for architecture, design and art. There is plenty of work by artists and designers associated with the Bauhaus, including paintings by Moholy-Nagy and Kandinsky, chairs by Marcel Breuer, Marianne Brandt's perfect little teapot, and original architectural drawings by Mies van der Rohe. First-rate temporary exhibitions are held in the main halls. You can also gain an insight into the teaching methods by viewing classroom assignments completed by students. Leave enough time to explore the excellent gift shop, which has stylish objects, from jewellery to carafes, all designed in the Bauhaus tradition. **Adm**

Neue Nationalgalerie *modern greats* `9 A1`

Potsdamer Strasse 50, Tiergarten • 030 26 62 65 1
» www.smb.spk-berlin.de/nng
Open 10–6 Tue, Wed & Fri, 10–10 Thu, 11–6 Sat & Sun

Designed in the 1960s by Mies van der Rohe, this glass temple deserves as much attention as the Picassos and Kandinskys on the walls inside. A base of paved granite is crowned by a glass cube, the transparent walls of which connect the interior space with the surrounding cityscape. The 2,500-sq-m (27,000-sq-ft) temporary exhibition space is coveted by contemporary artists; those who have shown here in recent years include Jenny Holzer, Ann Veronica Janssens and Douglas Gordon.

The permanent collection is housed in the building's lower level and leads the visitor through all the important developments of 20th-century art up to the 1970s. Its particular strength, however, is Modernism of the early 20th century. Picasso, De Chirico and Léger are all well represented, and the collection also

has rewarding examples by German Expressionists Ernst Ludwig Kirchner and Emil Nolde, as well as protagonists of *Neue Sachlichkeit* (New Objectivity) such as Otto Dix and Georg Grosz. There are also strong pieces from the postwar American generation, including Barnett Newman's 6-m (20-ft) painting *Who's Afraid of Red, Yellow, and Blue, 1969*.

The greatest living German artists Gerhard Richter, Rosemarie Trockel and Sigmar Polke are represented by key works. The most prominent painters of the former GDR, such as Werner Tübke, round out this part of the collection. Tübke paints scenes packed with hundreds of human figures in a style that draws heavily upon the Mannerism of the early 16th century.

A wall of windows along the lower level lures visitors outdoors to the calm retreat of a sculpture garden. Van der Rohe's elegant architectural elements create a unique outdoor museum that's home to abstract and figurative works by European artists – Renoir's *Large Washer Woman* is a particular delight. **Adm**

Gemäldegalerie *European painting*

9 A1

Matthäikirchplatz, Tiergarten • 030 26 62 95 1
>> www.smb.spk-berlin.de/gg
Open 10–6 Tue–Sun (to 10pm Thu)

The *grande dame* of Berlin's art collections contains many of the world's finest 13th–18th-century paintings. The collection is now housed in a modern purpose-built gallery in the Kulturforum, and is the central attraction of the complex. The strangely sloped approach to the Kulturforum completely obscures the buildings within, making the Gemäldegalerie difficult to locate from the street. However, the interior is very impressive, with high ceilings and natural lighting helping to show off the masterpieces at their best.

The paintings are arranged chronologically as well as geographically, with an especially strong collection of northern European masters. Among the Rembrandts and Van Eycks, don't miss the exquisite Miraflores Altarpiece by Flemish master Rogier van der Weyden or Vermeer's *Woman With a Pearl Necklace*. The works from Europe's southern regions include paintings by Giotto, Titian, Raphael (his *Madonna Terranuova* is especially lovely) and Correggio.

The galleries circle a striking inner courtyard, which conveniently allows access to any period room. Using the brochure map, available at the entrance, it is easy to find the museum's most popular works, such as Bruegel's *Netherlandish Proverbs*, and to quickly skirt over to Caravaggio's *Amor Victorious*, for example, or Velázquez's *Portrait of a Lady*. Botticelli's iconic *Venus Rising* is located in the downstairs study.

An excellent audio tour, in English and German only, is included in the admission charge. For respite, the cafés are on the Forum's upper level. **Adm**

Centre

Kaiser-Wilhelm-Gedächtnis-Kirche 8 F2

Breitscheidplatz, Charlottenburg • 030 21 85 02 3
» www.gedaechtniskirche.com
Open 9–7 daily; services 10am & 6pm Sun

If you've spent a hectic morning shopping along
Kurfürstendamm, the Kaiser Wilhelm Memorial Church
is a perfect stop for restoring some inner peace.

Following wartime damage, all that remains of the
Neo-Romanesque church of 1895 is the ravaged
church tower. It was preserved as a graphic reminder
of war's devastation and integrated into a concrete
and blue-stained-glass church designed by leading
Modernist architect Egon Eiermann.

The ruin of the "Hollow Tooth" (as the old building
was nicknamed) and Eiermann's 1961-built "Pillbox
and Lipstick" octagonal church hall and hexagonal bell
tower soon found their place in the hearts of Berliners
and visitors alike. The interior has a special atmosphere, as honeycomb-shaped stained-glass windows
illuminate the church hall with a calm blue light.

Museum für Fotografie *top snaps*   8 F1

Jebensstrasse 2, Charlottenburg • 030 26 63 66 6
» www.smb.spk-berlin.de Open 10–6 Tue–Sun (to 10pm Thu)

One thousand works by Helmut Newton and also
by his wife June are held here, along with personal
effects and the portrait photographer's customized
car, or "Newtonmobile". The marble staircase,
dominated by several "Big Nudes", leads to
temporary exhibitions upstairs. **Adm**

Museum Berggruen *modern masters*   1 B4

Schloss Strasse 1, Charlottenburg • 030 32 69 58 0
» www.smb.spk-berlin.de Open 10–6 Tue–Sun

This stunning collection is devoted to three of the most
popular modern artists of all time: Pablo Picasso, Henri
Matisse and Paul Klee. All Picasso's important periods
are covered, including *Portrait of Jaime Sabartes* from
the Blue Period, while among the Matisses are some
of the painter's famous late-period cut-outs. **Adm**

» *The Kulturforum complex includes art galleries, concert halls and theatres* (see p12)

Schloss Charlottenburg *old opulence* 1 B4

Spandauer Damm 22–4, Charlottenburg • 030 32 09 14 40
>> www.spsg.de Open 9–5 Tue–Sun

This splendid Prussian palace complex, severely damaged in World War II and since reconstructed, was built in 1695 as a relatively modest summer residence for Sophie Charlotte, the wife of Elector Frederick III. When Frederick became the first Prussian king in 1701, extensive additions were constructed, using Versailles in France as the model. In 1740 the king's grandson, Frederick the Great, commissioned a new east wing for his residence on an even grander scale and in a more lavish fashion.

The most interesting parts of the old palace are the ground-level apartments, but they are accessible only on a German-language guided tour (information sheets are available in English and French). Frederick's porcelain chamber, Sophie Charlotte's delicately hand-painted harpsichord and the ornate chapel are some of the highlights here.

The east wing can be toured with an audio guide (included in the ticket price) in several languages. Pride of place goes to the Golden Gallery, a 42-m (130-ft) long Rococo fantasy that would make the perfect backdrop for a Cinderella-type ball. Frederick the Great was a keen collector of 18th-century paintings. In his state apartments you'll find several major works by Watteau.

The Baroque grounds are lovely for a walk, even if you don't wish to visit the palace, and there is a pleasant restaurant in the Orangery. **Adm**

Bröhan-Museum *the taste-makers* 1 B4

Schloss Strasse 1a, Charlottenburg • 030 32 69 06 00
>> www.broehan-museum.de Open 10–6 Tue–Sun

Covering major design styles chronologically from 1890 to 1939, this vast private collection brings together exclusive examples of Art Nouveau, Art Deco and early Modernist design. Larger exhibits include a dining room by Peter Behrens and a Hector Guimard salon. Temporary exhibitions are also hosted. **Adm**

Centre & South

Olympiastadion *a venue for champions*
Olympischer Platz 3, Charlottenburg
030 30 25 00 23 22 • ⓢ Olympia-Stad
>> www.olympiastadion-berlin.de Tours 10–4 daily

Modernized to host the 2006 World Cup finals, this famous 1930s arena lost some of its historic atmosphere but gained a roof and comfortable seating. Scale the bell tower for a great view into the stadium and the adjacent Olympic pool. **Adm**

Deutsches Technikmuseum `9 B3`
Trebbiner Strasse 9 (main building)/Möckernstrasse 26 (Spectrum), Kreuzberg • 030 90 25 40
>> www.dtmb.de Open 9–5:30 Tue–Fri, 10–6 Sat & Sun

Everything from looms to locomotives and coal hods to computers are displayed at the enormous indoor and open-air complex of the Museum of Technology. The exhibits illuminate how the gadgets work, as well as their cultural significance.

The older main museum building is surrounded by a vast park with a brewery tower, windmill and freight train tracks. Topped by an original US bomber that dropped food supplies on West Berlin during the 1948 blockade, the new annexe houses the aerospace, navigation and architecture collection.

Young and old alike will also be delighted by the exhibits in the Spectrum, just across the street. Touching is actively encouraged, and fun, hands-on experiments teach the basic principles of how our world works and how we perceive it. **Adm**

Topographie des Terrors *Nazi history* `9 C1`
Niederkirchnerstrasse 8, Kreuzberg • 030 25 48 67 03
>> www.topographie.de Open 10–8 daily (to dusk Oct–Apr)

The architectural remains of the National Socialist centre of power provide the setting for a series of documentation panels (in German) and a free audio guide (German and English) that trace the history of Nazi terror. One of the few remaining sections of the Berlin Wall in its original location can also be seen here.

Art & Architecture

Jüdisches Museum *architectural genius* 9 D2

Lindenstrasse 9–14, Kreuzberg • 030 25 99 33 00
» www.jmberlin.de Open 10–10 Mon, 10–8 Tue–Sun

Presenting over 2,000 years of Jewish history and culture in Germany, this museum was founded in the 1970s with a modest exhibition in the Baroque building that today serves as the entrance hall to an extraordinary piece of contemporary architecture.

In 1989, the Polish-born architect Daniel Libeskind won an international competition to design the new Jewish Museum with his radical idea that the building itself could embody the ideas and emotions associated with the exhibits housed within it. The architect calls his zinc-clad creation "Between the Lines".

The most startling aspect of the building is its jagged shape. Seen from above, the outline can be likened to both a shattered Star of David and a bolt of lightning. Inside, the continuous, narrow, angular path through the museum symbolizes Jewish-Gentile relations,

while the final room is a "Void": an empty concrete space that signifies the eradication of Berlin's Jews in the Holocaust. The Holocaust Tower and Garden of Exile (a disorienting maze of concrete pillars) also make aspects of the Jewish experience palpable.

Libeskind's vision was realized in 1999 and attracted thousands of visitors even while it was still empty of displays. The permanent exhibition was installed in 2001 and tells the story of Jewish-German relations from ancient times to the present in 14 "chapters", using artifacts, models, drawings, photographs and a multimedia learning centre. Changing exhibitions highlight cultural themes, such as contemporary design in buildings with a Jewish function.

Past attacks on Jewish buildings in Germany have made tight security necessary – don't be put off by the body check at the entrance. Allow a whole day to take everything in, including a visit to the café, which has seating in the inner courtyard. **Adm**

Martin-Gropius-Bau *exhibition venue*   9 C1
Niederkirchnerstrasse 7, Kreuzberg • 030 25 48 60
>> www.gropiusbau.de Open 10–8 Wed–Mon

Named after its famous architect, the Martin-Gropius-Bau opened in 1881 as an arts and crafts museum. The brick building, which circles a spectacular central atrium, has been magnificently restored, and is now one of the best spaces in Berlin for exhibitions on anything from contemporary art to archaeology. **Adm**

Stasi Museum *secrets of the spies*
Ruschestrasse 103, Haus 1, Friedrichshain • ⓊMagdalenenstr.
>> www.stasi-museum.org Open 11–6 Mon–Fri, 2–6 Sat & Sun

The headquarters of the dreaded East German secret police, the Stasi, have been turned into a museum by members of the former GDR civil rights movement. The offices are supremely banal, but there is a fascinating range of spyware, such as Trabant car doors secretly equipped with infra-red communications devices. **Adm**

Mies van der Rohe Haus *sublime living*
Oberseestrasse 60, Hohenschönhausen
030 97 00 06 18 • Tram 27 or bus M5
>> www.miesvanderrohehaus.de
Open 1–6 Tue–Thu, 2–6 Sat & Sun

Also known as the Lemke House, this private country home was built by Mies van der Rohe for businessman Karl Lemke in 1932–3, after which the architect emigrated to the USA. Today it is a cultural heritage site. Although modest in comparison with the Neue Nationalgalerie *(see p77)*, which Van der Rohe built three decades later, it expresses the same Modernist ideals and signature floor-to-ceiling expanses of glass.

With its bright interiors, sleek parquet floors and unadorned white walls, the house is the perfect setting for exhibitions of contemporary art, which change four times a year. In summer you can walk through the glass doors out onto the back terrace. The renovated grounds appear to blend seamlessly into the Obersee lake and landscape beyond. **Adm**

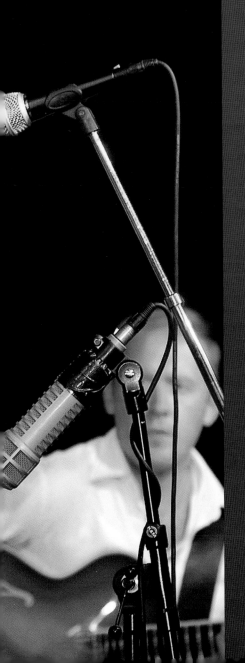

performance

Cutting-edge theatre and dance, and eclectic film screenings have long been associated with Berlin. Even the state-funded theatres – which include the Berliner Ensemble, founded in 1949 by Bertolt Brecht, and the new HAU theatres – stage politically charged drama. Music venues range from the Neo-Classical Konzerthaus am Gendarmenmarkt to modern rock arenas and smoky jazz clubs.

PERFORMANCE

For anyone interested in the stage and screen, Berlin offers a wealth of possibilities on any given evening – classical concerts, vaudeville-style entertainment, stand-up comedy, modern dance, art-house cinema and classics of the silver screen. The fringe theatre and cabaret scene is especially vibrant and bold, but the state-funded theatres too are socially and politically savvy – from the Berliner Ensemble, founded by Bertolt Brecht, to the experimental HAU theatres *(see p93)* in Kreuzberg.

Natalie Gravenor

Classical Concert Halls

The **Konzerthaus am Gendarmenmarkt** *(see p89)* offers a strong programme, while the **Staatsoper Unter den Linden** *(see p90)* expertly balances classical and modern opera, ballet and concert music – from Mozart to Pierre Boulez. The **Philharmonie** *(see p91)* is world-class, with state-of-the-art acoustics and a very fine orchestra.

Rock Venues

Young, unpretentious crowds flock to **Magnet Club** *(see p97)* for indie rock, while **Maria am Ufer** *(see p95)*, a former warehouse, hosts must-see live acts, DJs and multi-media events in a labyrinth of lounges, bars and performance spaces. Catch heavyweight international talent at the cavernous former bus depot **Arena Treptow** *(see p96)*.

Jazz Clubs

Berlin's jazz clubs offer plenty of atmosphere and great music from the international circuit. **Quasimodo** *(see p92)* has been going strong since the 1970s, and the smoky cellar remains a favourite with jazz musicians. **Yorckschlösschen** *(see p95)* is a cosy club and restaurant with garden seating, while upmarket **A-Trane** *(see p93)* hosts high profile jazz acts.

choice acts

Major Theatres

The Brecht-founded **Berliner Ensemble** *(see p88)* is the top choice for an evening of serious theatre. The **Volksbühne** *(see p90)* attracts an artsy-intellectual crowd with a sophisticated repertoire of socially critical and media-satirizing theatre, while the **Deutsches Theater** *(see p89)* packs in audiences with imaginative renditions of modern classics.

Independent Theatre and Cabaret

The **Sophiensäle** *(see p90)* centres on avant-garde theatre, dance and musical performances, while the **Bamah Jüdisches Theater** *(see p97)* presents original plays, revues and readings expressive of Jewish culture. In a city so closely associated with cabaret, **Tipi** *(see p97)* is the place to catch local stars Max Raabe, Gayle Tufts and Cora Frost.

Cinema

The **Arsenal** *(see p92)* is a mecca for cinemagoers with non-mainstream tastes, offering cinematic discoveries from every period, corner of the earth and genre. **Eiszeit** *(see p95)* shows a strong selection of international arthouse fare, while **Odeon** *(see p95)* specializes in original versions of Anglophone "quality" mainstream productions.

Berliner Ensemble, Theater am Schiffbauerdamm *house of Brecht*

`5 C2`

Bertolt-Brecht-Platz 1, Mitte • Box office 030 28 40 81 55
>> www.berliner-ensemble.de

This beautiful Neo-Baroque theatre (founded in 1892) is dubbed "BE" by locals. The "B" stands as much for the German playwright Bertolt Brecht as for Berliner. Brecht's *Threepenny Opera* premiered here in 1928, shocking audiences with its sardonic view of rampant capitalism in Weimar Germany, as seen through the sordid lives of beggars, thieves and prostitutes.

Exiled during World War II, Brecht returned to Berlin in 1949 and, together with his wife and creative partner, actress Helene Weigel, founded the Berliner Ensemble at the Deutsches Theater *(see opposite)*. A permanent home for the BE was made at the Theater am Schiffbauerdamm in 1954. Brecht died in 1956, since when a succession of diverse directors have imprinted their own style on BE.

BE is the venue of choice for an evening of erudite theatre. Brecht's works dominate the repertoire to this day, but there are also noteworthy (German-language) performances of famous plays by Shakespeare, Gotthold Ephraim Lessing, Friedrich Schiller, Henrik Ibsen and Samuel Beckett. Modern works include *Das Lebewohl (Les Adieux)* and others by recent Austrian Nobel Laureate Elfriede Jelinek, and *Oceanflight* by the American postmodern opera mastermind Robert Wilson. The visually complex multimedia collaborations with Wilson have received especially high praise.

In the participatory spirit of Brechtian theatre, some performances are followed by audience discussions with actors and directors in the plush upstairs lobby. The stars and star-struck alike mingle in the BE cafeteria, which serves typically hearty Berlin fare such as *Bouletten* (mincemeat patties). Shows at BE often sell out quickly (for ticket information, *see p91*).

Deutsches Theater and DT 5 B1
Kammerspiele *star-driven theatre classics*
Schumannstrasse 13a, Mitte • Box office 030 28 44 12 25
>> www.dt-berlin.de

Discerning theatregoers have been drawn to this
opulent Biedermeier-era building since 1850, though
its neon sign saying *"Verweil doch"* ("why not stay?"
– a partial quotation from Goethe) is a recent addition.

   In the 1920s, Max Reinhardt's innovative revivals
of established plays brought the house international
acclaim (and led to his illustrious Hollywood and
Broadway career). It was here, too, that Bertolt Brecht
and Helene Weigel founded the Berliner Ensemble
(see opposite). Under postwar Socialist rule, the
Deutsches Theater retained a mildly critical edge as
the crown jewel of the East Berlin theatres. Today, the
Deutsches Theater and the smaller Kammerspiele hall
offer imaginative renditions of modern classics starring
well-known faces of German stage and screen.
Occasional DJ sets cater to a hip crowd.

Konzerthaus am 5 D4
Gendarmenmarkt *classical music*
Gendarmenmarkt 2, Mitte • Box office 030 20 30 92 10 1
>> www.konzerthaus.de

Landmark events such as the Berlin premiere of
Beethoven's 9th were set in this grand Neo-Classical
hall before the bombs of World War II took their toll.
Reconstructed in 1984, it now offers a solid selection
of classical and new music concerts.

Avant-Garde Music

While not the centre of avant-garde arts that it
was in the 1920s, Berlin still nurtures a tradition
of experimental music. The world-renowned venue
Podewil has reopened as **Tesla** (Map 6 G3,
Klosterstr. 68–70, www.tesla-berlin.de), offering
concerts, audio art and sound installations.
So-called "new music" – which includes works by

relatively established composers such as John
Cage and Karlheinz Stockhausen – is performed
regularly at the **Konzerthaus** *(see above)* and every
Tuesday evening at **BKA Kreuzberg** (Map 9 C4,
Mehringdamm 32–4, www.unerhoerte-musik.de).
The **MaerzMusik** festival (www.maerzmusik.de),
which takes place in various locations in March,
showcases experimental acoustic works.

Performance

Staatsoper Unter den Linden
5 D3

Unter den Linden 7, Mitte • Box office 030 20 35 45 55
>> www.staatsoper-berlin.de

Israeli conductor Daniel Barenboim nurtures the 18th-century opera house's long tradition of balancing classical with modern. Expect Mozart and Wagner to rub shoulders with Pierre Boulez and electronica DJs. The Apollosaal hall regularly hosts club events and is one of the PopComm Music Festival venues (see p18).

Sophiensäle *avant-garde performance art*   6 E1

Sophienstrasse 18, Mitte • Box office 030 28 35 26 6
>> www.sophiensaele.com

The Sophiensäle, opened in 1996, is a child of the post-reunification creative spirit that has shaped the Mitte-Scheunenviertel district. Choreographer Sasha Waltz has helped to establish the theatre's reputation for avant-garde theatre, dance and musical performances with a twist of absurd humour.

Volksbühne *challenging theatre*   4 F3

Linienstrasse 227, Mitte • Box office 030 24 06 57 77
>> www.volksbuehne-berlin.de Box office noon–6pm daily

True to its name of "people's stage", the main branch of the Volksbühne (full name: Volksbühne am Rosa-Luxemburg-Platz) is easy to locate thanks to the oversized OST ("east") sign on its façade and huge, two-legged wheel sculpture on the lawn. However, the dramatic fare that theatre director Frank Castorf serves is not always mass entertainment: rather it is an often volatile mixture of modern drama and TV soap opera, biographical dance theatre and confrontational political commentaries. The Volksbühne also regularly hosts rock and electronica concerts, club nights and themed events with music, films and talks centring on pop or political issues.

Flanking the main stage, the smaller Roter Salon hall hosts electronica, drum 'n' bass, indie and soul DJ nights. Another hall, the Grüner Salon, is one of the best venues in Germany for swing dancing.

Philharmonie & Kammermusiksaal `9 B1`

Herbert-von-Karajan-Strasse 1, Tiergarten
Box office 030 25 48 80
>> www.berliner-philharmoniker.de

The erection of the Wall in 1961 turned the area around Potsdamer Platz – formerly Europe's busiest urban space – into a cultural wasteland. However, the West Berlin authorities had ambitions to revitalize their side of the neighbourhood with new buildings for cultural institutions, including the Philharmonie. A daringly modern concert hall designed by Hans Scharoun opened in 1963. Conceived primarily for the ear, not the eye, this peculiarly assymetrical, tent-like building revolutionized concert-hall acoustics.

The chamber music hall (Kammermusiksaal) next door, also based on Scharoun's ideas, was completed in 1987 by Edgar Wisniewski. Having re-invented itself under its chief conductor, Sir Simon Rattle, the house orchestra, the Berliner Philharmoniker, is now regarded as being among the finest in the world.

Buying Theatre Tickets

High-profile productions tend to sell out very quickly in Berlin. The cheapest, but most time-consuming way to purchase tickets is to go along in person to the theatre box office, and wait in line. Most major theatres also now offer the facility to buy or reserve tickets on their websites, which is a slightly more expensive option, but good for short-term visitors whose time is limited. However, the theatre websites offer no more guarantee of availability than their box offices.

The largest commercial website offering tickets for a wide range of events is **www.eventim.de**, which charges a hefty commission. Official city website **www.berlin.de** offers tickets for same-day events (under the category "Kultur & Tickets"). Tickets for popular concerts and performances are also often auctioned (usually without any legal restrictions) on **eBay**. Commercial box offices such as **Interklassik** (Map 5 C3, Friedrichstr. 90, at the Dussmann Kulturkaufhaus, 030 20 16 60 93) or **Ars Scribendi** (Map 5 A5, Potsdamer Platz Arkaden, Alte Potsdamer Str. 7, 030 25 29 69 87) often have tickets for otherwise sold-out shows, but they charge additional fees of up to 20% of the original ticket price. The two **Hekticket** shops (one at Hardenbergstr. 29d, in the lobby of Deutsche Bank Charlottenburg, Map 8 F1, 030 23 09 93 0 for last-minute sales, or 030 23 09 33 3 for advance sales; the other at the Alexanderplatz train station entrance, Karl-Liebknecht-Str. 12, Map 6 G2, 030 24 31 24 31) charge less commission and offer same-day tickets at half-price. You can also reserve online at **www.hekticket.de** and pick the tickets up at one of the shops (payment must be in cash).

If all else fails, you can always show up an hour before showtime at the theatre and hope that someone returns their tickets.

Performance

Theater am Potsdamer Platz `9 B1`
Marlene-Dietrich-Platz 1, Tiergarten • 01805 44 44
>> www.stageholding.de

Italian architect Renzo Piano's nine-storey landmark, centred on an impressive, 1,800-seat theatre, was completed in 1998. It has hosted musicals such as *Cats* and high-profile performers such as The Blue Man Group. Its Adagio club and Berlin Film Festival in February *(see p19)* attract a glamorous crowd.

Arsenal *national cinematheque theatre* `5 A5`
Potsdamer Strasse 2 (in basement of Filmhaus/Sony Center), Tiergarten • 030 26 95 51 00
>> www.fdk-berlin.de

Its location in one of Berlin's most commercial districts belies the Arsenal's radical origins. It was founded in the early 1970s by the Friends of the German Cinematheque, an organization that supports the state film archive and also propagates experimental and political cinema. The first Arsenal became a mecca for cinema-goers with non-mainstream tastes, showing everything from American underground cinema to Soviet silent classics (such as *Arsenal* by Aleksandr Dovzhenko, which inspired the theatre's name).

In 2001 Arsenal moved into the basement of the Sony Center, adding a second screen that shows movie milestones from the silent era to today, often in the original version with German subtitles. Both screens stay true to Arsenal's roots, offering cinematic discoveries from every corner of the world.

Quasimodo *Europe's smokiest juke joint* `8 E1`
Kantstrasse 12a, Charlottenburg • 030 31 28 08 6
>> www.quasimodo.de
Café open from noon daily, showtime from 10pm

Since the 1970s, this cellar club has been the preferred port of call for jazz and guitar-based rock artists. Internationally renowned acts like fusion saxman Bill Evans or hip-hop poetess Me'shell Ndegeocello appear alongside local talent.

For the very latest on Berlin go to >> www.realcity.dk.com

World Music

Berlin's live music scene reflects the city's multicultural nature. The most high-profile venue is the **Haus der Kulturen der Welt** *(see p75)*, which regularly stages folk, pop and fusion acts. This is also home to the **Multikulti** radio station (FM 96.3), which spins records from all over the world and offers shows in 18 languages.

Werkstatt der Kulturen (Map 10 G5, Wissmannstr. 31–42, Neukölln, www.werkstatt-der-kulturen.de) acts as a community centre for musicians and organizes the **Karneval der Kulturen** festival *(see p16)*, which attracts over a million visitors each year. **Kesselhaus** (Map 4 F1, Kulturbrauerei complex, www.kesselhaus-berlin.de) is especially good for music from Central and Eastern Europe.

A-Trane *upscale jazz club* `8 E1`
Bleibtreustrasse 1, Charlottenburg • 030 31 32 55 0
>> www.a-trane.de Open from 9pm daily

This studiously stylish jazz club in a lively, upscale neighbourhood appeals to the over-35 crowd. Reserve tickets for shows with big names like German trumpeter Till Brönner or US rock-jazz crossover star Curtis Stigers. Bebop trombonist Tony Hurdle has also played many gigs here.

Hebbel am Ufer (HAU) `9 C2`
HAU 1: Stresemannstrasse 29, Kreuzberg (Map 9 C2)
HAU 2: Hallesches Ufer 32, Kreuzberg (Map 9 C3)
HAU 3: Tempelhofer Ufer 10, Kreuzberg (Map 9 C3)
>> www.hau-berlin.de • Box office 030 25 90 04 27

In 2003, three theatres in a moribund Kreuzberg neighbourhood were merged to create the Hebbel am Ufer, or HAU (aptly, the German word for "hit"). The merger, a move to cut costs, actually released a massive creative energy under the direction of Matthias Lilienthal, who used to be at Volksbühne *(see p90)*. The three HAU venues are now popular for challenging theatre by independent groups from many countries. HAU's programme includes film, pop music, lectures, dance and avant-garde drama, and most productions are in German.

All three of the HAU theatres have lobby lounges, which have become popular hangouts for Berlin's young arty crowd. HAU 2's lobby is especially popular for aftershow DJ sets and parties.

Schaubühne *contemporary dance & drama* `7 B3`

Kurfürstendamm 153, Charlottenburg • Box office 030 89 00 23
»» www.schaubuehne.de

The Schaubühne Ensemble was founded in 1962 in
the working-class West Berlin district of Kreuzberg.
Inspired by the politically charged climate of the
1960s and early 70s, and wanting to offer an
alternative to German state theatre, Schaubühne's
director in those turbulent times, Peter Stein, sought
to break down the barriers between director and
player, emphasizing creative equality. This fresh
approach soon led to acclaimed interpretations
of a diverse repertoire, from Greek tragedy and
Shakespeare to prominent dramatists of the 1970s,
such as Botho Strauss and Peter Handke.

In 1981 the Ensemble moved to a former cinema
designed by Modernist architect Erich Mendelsohn
in the more bourgeois district of Wilmersdorf. The round
building was revamped by Jürgen Sawade to become
the best-equipped theatre in Germany at that time.
Schaubühne continued to captivate and provoke
theatregoers and in 1999 scooped up the leading
lights of East Berlin's cutting-edge performing arts:
directors Thomas Ostermeier and Jens Hillje from the
Deutsches Theater *(see p89)*, post-modern
choreographer Sasha Waltz from the Sophiensäle
(see p90) and her creative partner, Jochen Sandig.

Since then, modern dance and drama have formed
the core of Schaubühne's repertoire. There is always
a bold choice of contemporary material, for example
Waltz's *S* and *Insideout* dances (knowledge of the
German language not essential), as well as topical
interpretations of classic plays, such as Henrik
Ibsen's *A Doll's House* (called *Nora* in Germany).
Especially recommended – if your German's good
enough – are the harrowing works by the late
British playwright Sarah Kane, including *Zerbombt*
(*Blasted*) and *4:48 Psychose* (*4:48 Psychosis*).

Eiszeit *eclectic film programme* `10 H2`

Zeughof Strasse 20, Kreuzberg • 030 61 16 01 6
>> www.eiszeit-kino.de

Having established itself as an international art-house cinema in the 1980s, Eiszeit is now known for screening everything from ambitious auteur films to formulaic splatter movies, all usually undubbed, with German subtitles. Turkish films and children's matinees are strong on the programme too.

Yorckschlösschen *cosy jazz club* `9 C4`

Yorckstrasse 15, Kreuzberg • 030 21 58 07 0
>> www.yorckschloesschen.de Open from 9am daily

For over 100 years, this venue has been the focus of life on an otherwise unprepossessing residential street connecting Kreuzberg and Schöneberg. Don't expect big-league or avant-garde jazz, but mellow trad sounds as part of an overall relaxing experience. There is a restaurant and a lovely beer garden too.

Odeon/Babylon *old-fashioned cinemas* `8 H5`

Odeon: Hauptstrasse 116, Schöneberg • 030 78 70 40 19
Babylon: Dresdenerstrasse 126, Kreuzberg • 030 61 60 96 93
>> www.yorck.de

A cinema from yesteryear, complete with marquee, the Odeon shows mainly mainstream English-language films. Sister cinema Babylon (Map 10 F1) usually has more offbeat international fare, undubbed. Home-made brownies are sold at both.

Columbiahalle/club *rock and pop gigs* `9 D5`

Columbiadamm 13–21, Tempelhof • 030 69 80 98 0
>> www.columbiahalle.de / www.columbiaclub.de

The 3,500-capacity Columbiahalle and smaller Columbiaclub next door are two of Berlin's major rock venues. The Halle hosts arena-filling stars such as New Order and The White Stripes, while indie acts such as the Stereophonics or soulful Eurovision entrant Max Mutzke grace the Club's stage.

Maria am Ufer *intriguing nightclub* `10 H1`

Stralauer Platz 34–5, Friedrichshain • 030 21 23 81 90
>> www.clubmaria.de Opening times vary

If you're into electronica and indie music, this riverside club should be on your agenda. The former warehouse has been transformed into a labyrinth of lounges, bars and performance spaces. Imaginative lighting, a booming sound system and multi-media effects support the must-see live acts and DJ nights.

Arena Treptow riverside complex   `11 B4`

Eichenstrasse 4, Treptow • Box office 030 53 32 03 85/6
>> www.arena-berlin.de

Like many entertainment venues that have opened in East Berlin since 1989, Arena has filled an obsolete commercial building (in this case a bus depot) and helped to revitalize a dull district. It is now the city's largest non-sports indoor entertainment venue, staging megastar concerts by the likes of British trip-hop band Massive Attack and hit productions such as the comedy *Caveman*.

The riverside around the stadium has also been developed. The complex now includes the Glashaus theatre and club, Magazin gallery and the Arena Badeschiff *(see p137)* – a huge swimming pool set on a docked ship on the Spree. A limited range of food and drink is available at all these locations, but a better menu is found at a restaurant in the docked riverboat *MS Hoppetosse,* which is also a popular venue for reggae and soul parties.

Knaack Club live music and DJ sets   `4 H1`

Greifswalder Strasse 224, Prenzlauer Berg • 030 44 27 06 0/1
>> www.knaack-berlin.de Open from 9pm

The various youth subcultures of Berlin gather at this backstreet venue, depending on the theme of the night. Punk, alternative, electro, synthpop and nu-metal are played live or off the turntables on four grungy floors. Ticket prices are moderate, even for the well-known acts.

Bastard quirky venue for rock & electronica   `4 F1`

Kastanienallee 7–9, Prenzlauer Berg • 030 44 04 96 69
>> www.clubbastard.de Opening times vary

Located on the premises of the Prater beergarden and a small offshoot of the Volksbühne *(see p90)*, Bastard (yes, that's the name) is worth a visit, if only to read its walls plastered with trashy magazines or to sit on an old sofa with a beer. The poetry slams, indie rock and electronica sets are the icing on the cake.

Magnet Club *guitar-driven indie shows* `4 H1`
Greifswalder Str. 212–13, Prenzlauer Berg • 030 44 00 81 40
>> www.magnet-club.de Open from 8pm daily

After the jazz club Miles folded on this site, Magnet soon established itself as a popular venue for a young indie crowd thanks to a booking policy that mixes promising local newcomers with well-known German bands such as Fehlfarben. Live acts perform in the back, while the front room houses a comfortable lounge and bar.

Bamah Jüdisches Theater
Jonasstrasse 22 • 030 25 11 09 6 • ⓤ Leinestrasse
>> www.bamah.de

When Bamah (Hebrew for "stage") opened in 2001, it was the first "Jewish" theatre in Berlin for over 60 years. As director Dan Lahav explains, "Jewish" does not necessarily mean theatre by Jews for Jews, rather that the theatre is open to anyone interested in Jewish culture and engaging in dialogue about it.

After establishing itself in Wilmersdorf, Bamah then took over the defunct Steinplatz cinema in 2004 and has since moved to new premises in the south-east of the city. The company's repertoire includes original plays, revues and tributes to important Jewish cultural figures, such as painter Marc Chagall and composer Friedrich Holländer (of *Falling In Love Again* fame). Other performances might tackle issues of conflict, such as that between faith and sexuality explored in *The Rebbe and the Transvestite*.

Cabaret in Berlin Today
In the 1920s, Berlin was famous for shocking avant-garde cabaret acts. A sanitized and highly enjoyable version, called *Varieté*, can be found at the **Wintergarten** (Map 5 A5, Potsdamer Str. 96, www.wintergarten-berlin.de), **Chamäleon** (Map 6 F1, Rosenthaler Str. 40–41, www.chamaeleon-variete.de), **Bar Jeder Vernunft** (Map 8 F2, Schaperstr. 24, www.bar-jeder-vernunft.de) and **Tipi** (Map 3 A4, Grosse Querallee, www.tipi-das-zelt.de). Popular acts on the circuit include diva Cora Frost and 30s-style crooner Max Raabe.

What Germans call *Kabarett* is really a form of stand-up comedy, such as the government-mocking *When Thierse Rings Twice* show staged at **Distel** (Map 5 C4, Friedrichstr. 101, www.distel-berlin.de).

bars & clubs

Berliners certainly know how to party, and their city's nightlife is arguably now the liveliest in Europe. Bars and clubs in many districts hire talented home-grown and international DJs to help keep the revelry going through the night. Electroclash, hip-hop, rock, soca, salsa and just about every other form of dance music new and old is found in this city. Some bars are open in daytime too, serving food and drink almost around the clock.

BARS & CLUBS

Diverse and unique are the words that best describe Berlin's nightlife scene, which makes the most of the city's tumultous history and idiosyncratic urban landscape. Where else can one sip cocktails near the former no-man's-land then dance to techno beat amidst the vestiges of Socialist-era architecture? Compared to other European capitals, going out in Berlin is a democratic pastime too – drink prices remain moderate and bars and clubs have a greater sense of camaraderie than exclusivity.

Natalie Gravenor

Gay and Lesbian Haunts

Berlin has long been a gay haven, with the scene's institutions, such as café-bar **Bierhimmel** *(see p111)*, coexisting happily with newcomers like cocktail bar **Sharon Stonewall** *(see p108)*, which welcomes a broad mix of gays, lesbians and straights. **Black Girls Coalition** *(see p117)* hosts gender- and genre-bending parties, mixing punk, electroclash and drag.

Cult Bars

Club der Polnischen Versager *(see p105)* is where the Polish expat community meets. **Gagarin** *(see p119)* is a bar-restaurant with a Soviet Space-Age theme, offering Russian dishes and Baltika beer. Pre-1989 East boho haunt **Kaffee Burger** *(see p105)* has gained cult status through its offbeat programme of live acts and DJ sets.

Retro Music Clubs

With everything old becoming new again, dance clubs such as **Bohannon** *(see p102)* – named after funk great Hamilton Bohannon – are happily embracing musical styles of the past. Small but popular **Konrad Tönz** *(see p114)* recalls the 70s in decor and music, while floor-filling DJs spin reliable oldies at the spacious **Frannz Club** *(see p121)*.

choice nightlife

Techno and Electronica Clubs

Berlin has always been at the forefront of the techno and electronica scene. **Sternradio** *(see p103)* offers an East Berlin retro-chic backdrop for top DJs. The steady beat of house, electro and techno grooves emanates from **Watergate** *(see p111)*, and **Berghain** *(see p117)* attracts growing crowds for cutting-edge electronic sounds and visuals.

Top Cocktail Bars

The Caipirinha has settled alongside beer as the prefered Berlin drink. This and other cocktails can be sampled at the excellent **Bar am Lützowplatz** *(see p108)*. Schöneberg's **Green Door** *(see p116)* offers top-notch cocktails in a cooly elegant ambience, while the **Haifischbar** *(see p114)*, in funkier Kreuzberg, serves cocktails and delicious sushi.

Worldbeat Clubs

Berlin is catching up with Paris and London as a centre for worldbeat. **Havanna** *(see p116)* offers salsa and merengue. **Lumumba** *(see p104)* is a cramped but friendly meeting place for aficionados of Afro-Caribbean and African grooves – from highlife to zouk and salsa. The **Mudd Club** *(see p107)* is a hub for Balkan Beats and Bollywood scores.

Bohannon *cool club* 6 F1

Dircksenstrasse 40, Mitte • 030 69 50 52 87

>> www.bohannon.de Open from 10pm Mon, Thu, Sat & Sun

This fairly recent addition to the nightlife landscape has injected some much-needed street cred into the tourist-trap mile of clubs clustered around Hackescher Markt. An illustrious and eclectic cross-section of international and local DJ crews lay down the tracks for the club nights – from reggae and dancehall institution Barney Millah's Escobar (every Monday) to Jazzanova's occasional chillout sets. Funk and electronic live acts spice up the programme, and the Bohannon is also said to host secret gigs by big names (subscribe to their newsletter at info@bohannon.de and maybe you will privy to who's next). Tribute is paid to the club's namesake – 70s Motown bandleader and disco-funk pioneer Hamilton Bohannon – at the "Thank God It's Friday" parties, where a friendly (but not pushy) thirtyish crowd bumps and grinds to the disco stompers of their early youth.

Much care has been put into making Bohannon a pleasant hangout as well as dancefloor experience. The decor skilfully treads the fine line between underground charm and classiness, its leather furniture paired with bare brick walls. The bar boasts a selection of well-mixed standards and speciality cocktails, snacks and the popular (but hard to get in Berlin) Jamaican brew Red Stripe. If you tire of dancing and have not yet found someone to chat with, the table football is a great way to score some goals and some engaging conversation.

Sage Club *funky parties, hiphop and house* `6 H5`
Köpenicker Strasse 76, Mitte • 030 27 89 83 0
>> www.sage-club.de Opening times vary; check website

The labyrinthine Sage Club, located directly under the Heinrich-Heine-Strasse U-bahn station, began life as a hiphop club called Boogaloo while the Berlin Wall was crumbling. Since then, the musical offerings have widened to include house, electro funk and even indie rock. The crowds have become more extravagant in recent years, which might have something to do with Berlin drag star Gerome Castell now being on the management. Sage's door staff are discerning, so leave your sports shoes at home unless they go with expensive Tommy Hilfiger homeboy gear.

There are four contrasting nights each week: Thursday is for rock music; Friday for rhythm and soul; Saturday for international house; Sunday for a mix of dance music. In summer, Sage goes overground with beach parties and barbecues in a garden behind the U-bahn station entrance.

Café Moskau/KMA 36 *bar and venue* `6 H2`
Karl-Marx-Allee 34 & 36, Mitte • 030 24 63 16 26
Bar open 6:30pm–2am Sun–Thu, 6:30pm–6am Fri & Sat

The Café Moskau and neighbouring KMA 36 bar are set within a GDR-era building with wooden panelling and glass façades. Café Moskau is more a lounge bar with a dance floor for party nights and special events than a café. The cramped KMA 36 bar also puts on live pop acts and electronica DJ sets.

Sternradio *techno and house club* `6 G2`
Alexanderplatz 5, Mitte • 030 24 62 59 32 0
>> www.sternradio-berlin.de Opening times vary; check website

Named after a transistor radio made in the former GDR, this club nurtures its East German retro-futurist image. Fun gimmicks include TV monitors that broadcast the drinks list. Top DJs play techno and house sets — at weekends, you can listen in online at www.klubradio.de.

>> *East German retro-futurism is a popular theme in East Berlin bars – see also Gagarin p119*

Lumumba *African and Caribbean music* `4 G4`
Karl-Marx-Allee 35, Mitte • 0173 98 60 06 4
Open from 8pm Tue–Thu, from 11pm Fri & Sat

The Lumumba club reflects Berlin's growing African diaspora community and interest in music from south of the Sahara. Located near the International Cinema, Café Moskau and KMA 36 *(see p103)*, Lumumba has helped to turn this previously unspectacular residential area of Mitte (characterized by prefab high-rises) into a small hub of nightlife.

The style of music known as highlife (a kind of African jazz) is well represented. Caribbean zouk is also popular, its energy and rhythms bearing traces of many other styles, including salsa. Wednesday nights feature reggae. The crowd is a mix of African expats and other Berliners, with an unusually broad age range – from teenagers to 40-somethings. The atmosphere is friendly, and there is a good range of drinks, including affordable cocktails.

While Lumumba is the only African dance club in Mitte, there are others outside the city centre, especially in Kreuzberg and Schöneberg. Try the **Mandingo Afro Night Club** (Map 9 C4, Mehringdamm 107), **Tam Tam** (Map 10 H3, Wiener Strasse 34, www.tam-tam-afrodisco.de), the **Village** (Map 8 H3, Frankenstr. 13) or the **Roots Afro Caribbean Bar** (Map 8 F2, Nürnberger Str. 17). Like Lumumba, most others freely mix reggae and Trinidadian soca with their African musical cousins. For information about events in Germany's African communities, check the German-language website www.cybernomads.net or listen to the world music station Radio Multikulti *(see p93)*.

Club der Polnischen Versager `4 F3`

Torstrasse 66, Mitte • 030 28 09 37 79
>> www.polnischeversager.de Open from 9pm daily

Run by Polish expats – a growing section of Berlin's population – this small, salon-like club now also attracts a large non-Polish following besides the expats. The "Club of Polish Losers", as it is called, regularly hosts art exhibitions, readings, film screenings (with English or German subtitles) and concerts. Most have a Polish theme, though you might also catch animated films from Estonia or musical offerings by the Berlin-based Don't Shelest, a Polish crossover punk band.

Membership of the club is mandatory, but easily obtainable upon purchase of your first drink. Polish and German beers are available. If you enjoy the music, check out the Pigasus gallery a few doors down (Torstr. 60), which sells East European CDs, including some by bands that perform at the club, alongside a range of Polish posters and prints.

Kaffee Burger *cutting-edge venue* `4 F3`

Torstrasse 60, Mitte • 030 28 04 64 95
>> www.kaffeeburger.de
Open from 7pm Sun–Thu, from 9pm Fri & Sat

The eclectic programme at this long-standing boho club includes live music by local and East European acts, and DJs spinning anything from "crimejazz" to East Berlin punk. It also hosts Vladimir Kaminer's legendary bi-monthly Saturday "Russian Disco".

King Kong Klub *quirky bar and club* `4 E2`

Brunnenstrasse 173, Mitte • 030 91 20 68 60
>> www.king-kong-klub.de
Open from 9pm nightly (performance times vary)

This friendly bar with a small stage and dance floor offers live and recorded music from the more far-flung regions of the pop world, such as Britain in the 1980s, Eastern Europe, and South and East Asia. There are occasional readings too. Drinks are reasonably priced.

Bars & Clubs

Z-Bar *bar for horror movie addicts*

3 D2

Bergstrasse 2, Mitte • 030 28 38 91 21
➤➤ www.z-bar.de Open from 8pm nightly

One of many trendy bars in the Mitte district, the Z-Bar is distinguished from the rest by the cult status of its back room. Here, TV junkies can get their fix on Friday and Sunday evenings with offerings from the Hammer House of Horror and programmes with titles such as *The Dark Side of Children's Television*.

Rio *attention-grabbing electro club*

3 C2

Chausseestrasse 106, Mitte
➤➤ www.rioberlin.de Opening times vary; check website

Projected graffiti tags help create a funky urban feel at this ultra-hip club that's often mentioned in the music press. It's the favourite hangout of Berlin-based singer Peaches. A variety of sounds from Bollywood tunes to the 80s retro style called electroclash keeps the friendly, 30-ish crowd grooving on the dance floor.

Berlin's Lounges

Lounge bars in Berlin range from gritty to ritzy. Into the first category fall locations such as **Verein der Visionäre**, a bar near the Landwehrkanal (Map 11 A4, off Schlesische Str.), the **X-Bar** in Prenzlauer Berg (Raumerstr. 30) and the arty **Erdbeerbar** in Mitte (Map 6 F1, Max-Beer-Str. 56). If you like grottoes, try **Arcanoa** in Kreuzberg (Map 9 C4, Am Tempelhofer Berg 8, www.arcanoa.de), which offers cool music and film screenings, and is a favourite with people from former Yugoslavia.

Progressively more upscale are **Scotch & Sofa** (Map 4 G1, Kollwitzstrasse 18, Prenzlauer Berg), the over-designed but popular **Seven Lounge** (Map 3 D2, Ackerstrasse 20) and the high-powered **Newton Bar** on the Gendarmenmarkt square (Map 5 D4, Charlottenstrasse 57). The **Josty Bar** in the Sony Center (Map 5 A5, www.josty-berlin.de) has an interesting glass façade that incorporates parts of the old grand hotel Esplanade. Its front lounge is atmospheric, with lots of dark wood and leather seats, but the cocktails are quite pricey.

An interesting variant is the **Orient Lounge** (Map 10 F2, above the Rote Harfe bar, Oranienstrasse 13), in the heart of Turkish Kreuzberg. The upstairs lounge here is like a scene from the *Thousand and One Nights*, with individual booths, and floor seating on thick carpets and lavishly embroidered cushions. Hookahs with various types of tobacco are on offer alongside wine, tea, non-alcoholic beverages and Turkish delicacies.

Increasingly, Berlin's nightclubs are creating lounge areas away from the dance floor (still called chillout zones in some techno clubs), where revellers can relax and converse with each other. Indeed, clubs such as **Matrix** *(see p118)* and **Café Moskau** *(see p103)* devote as much care to the design of their lounges as to the sound system.

Ambulance Bar *top-notch drinks & DJ sets* `5 D1`
Oranienburger Strasse 27, Mitte • 030 28 12 09 5
>> www.ambulancebar.de Open from 6pm nightly

This stylish lounge bar in the Scheunenviertel *(see p125)* is located on a buzzing street that's popular with tourists as well as locals. The upper stratum of Berlin's DJ scene rubs shoulders with new talent at the turntables, providing either funky or housey tracks. The cocktails are a bit pricey but well mixed.

Kilkenny Irish Pub `6 E2`
Hackescher Markt (in S-Bahn station), Mitte • 030 28 32 08 4
Open 10am–2am Mon–Thu & Sun, 10am–4am Fri & Sat

An award-winning Irish pub set into the arches of the Hackescher Markt station, Kilkenny is popular with native Berliners, the city's small Irish community and tourists from around the world. Drinks revolve around the Kilkenny brew (a mild Irish ale), cider and German beers. Shepherd's pie, crisps and football matches shown on the TV help to round out the Irish pub experience. You can relax on the velvet upholstered chairs or in wooden booths inside, or, in summer, there is outdoor seating on the small patch of green between the station and tram stop.

Note that, unlike in Ireland, service is generally at the table, and if you sit outside, you are obliged to pay the friendly, if sometimes overstretched, staff for each round. Over in Charlottenburg are two offshoots: the **Irish Harp** (Map 7 D2, Giesebrechtstrasse 15) and **Irish Pub** (Map 8 G2, Europa-Center).

Mudd Club *revival of New York legend* `6 E1`
Grosse Hamburger Str. 17 (in courtyard), Mitte • 030 44 03 62 99
>> www.muddclub.de Opening hours vary; check website

New York's Mudd Club of the early 1980s was a mecca of New Wave nightclubbing. The Berlin reincarnation (created by the same man who ran the NYC club) offers international indie acts, Balkan beats and Bollywood tunes, attracting a student to 30-something mixed gay and straight crowd. The beer is cheap.

Bars & Clubs

Sophienclub *straightforward dance club* `6 E1`
Sophienstrasse 6, Mitte • 0173 21 53 04 0
>> www.sophienclub-berlin.de Open from 10pm Tue–Sat

A young, mixed crowd packs out the two dance floors of this former East Berlin youth club. Downstairs, the focus is on hip-hop and R 'n' B, while upstairs there is usually a well-assembled mix of chart hits, disco classics, indie and Britpop. Prepare for an evening of non-stop dancing – seats are few and far between.

Sharon Stonewall *gay & lesbian hangout* `5 C1`
Linienstrasse 136, Mitte • 030 24 08 55 02
>> www.sharonstonewall.de Open from 8pm nightly

Attentive bar staff skilfully mix the cocktails at this small but busy bar. The pink interior and the name (a fusion of lesbian icon Sharon Stone and the legendary bar in NYC's Greenwich Village) indicate a gay slant, but the bar is actually very welcoming to all. There are occasional DVD screenings of camp classics.

Felix *classy place for networking* `5 B4`
Behrenstrasse 72, Mitte • 030 20 62 86 0
>> www.felixrestaurant.de Open 6pm–3am Wed–Sat

The glitzy Hotel Adlon Kempinski *(see p148)* is the venue for this restaurant-cum-club. Felix caters to an upmarket crowd seeking refined dining, civilized partying and, most of all, an evening of social networking. Wednesday night is the time to come for genteel jazz sounds; Saturday is disco night.

Bar am Lützowplatz *classy cocktails* `8 H2`
Lützowplatz 7, Tiergarten • 030 26 26 80 7
>> www.baramluetzowplatz.com Open 2pm–4am daily

Ignore the tourist traps on nearby Potsdamer Platz in favour of a quiet drink here, especially if you're on your way to Trompete *(see opposite)*. You'll find Berlin's longest bar and arguably the city's best cocktails, including Champagne mixes. The drinks are relatively inexpensive for such a posh location.

Trompete *grown-up meeting place* `8 H2`

Lützowplatz 9, Tiergarten • 030 23 00 47 94
➤➤ www.trompete-berlin.de
Open from 7pm Thu, from 10pm Fri & Sat

This stylish, if slightly impersonal club can be hit and miss in terms of programme quality and vibe, but the after-work parties on Thursdays have become an institution. Come if you want to mingle with a vaguely hip, 30- to 40-something crowd of Berliners.

Victoria Bar *upscale watering hole* `9 A2`

Potsdamer Strasse 102, Tiergarten • 030 25 75 99 77
➤➤ www.victoriabar.de
Open 6:30pm–3am Sun–Thu, 6:30pm–4am Fri & Sat

The Victoria's chic interior, with wooden panelling and modern art prints, has received many plaudits. More importantly, however, the bar cultivates an inviting atmosphere and has an extensive cocktail list, which makes it popular with a regular band of locals.

Paris Bar & Le Bar du Paris Bar `8 E1`

Kantstrasse 152–3, Charlottenburg • 030 31 38 05 2
➤➤ www.parisbar.de Paris Bar open noon–2am daily;
Le Bar du Paris Bar open from 5pm nightly

Charlottenburg's chi-chi Paris Bar established its reputation as a favourite haunt of the rich and famous in the decade after World War II. Even though in recent years the main focus of Berlin's glitterati has shifted eastwards to locations such as Borchardt *(see p28)* near Gendarmenmarkt, the Parisian-style brasserie and bar still attracts politicians, artists and others. Despite filing for bankruptcy in 2006, the bar continues to operate – the menu features decent, but not awe-inspiring, French cuisine.

Somewhat confusingly, right next door to the Paris Bar is its sister operation, Bar du Paris Bar. It is open only in the evening and is a good place if you just want to drink and have a snack before heading off elsewhere else. The extensive bar list includes cognacs and cocktails.

Abraxas *popular singles' club* `8 E1`
Kantstrasse 134, Charlottenburg • 030 31 29 49 3
Open usually from 10pm Wed–Sat; phone for details

Nearing its third decade, Abraxas has always been a reliable bet for those who like a bit of flirtation in the evening. The tiny dance floor is usually packed, so body contact is inevitable. Carlos Santana's *Abraxas* tracks are not played as often as they used to be, but the music is still heavily Latin and funk-flavoured.

Big Eden *from tacky to hip* `8 E2`
Kurfürstendamm 202, Charlottenburg • 030 88 26 12 0
>> www.big-eden.de Open from 11pm Thu–Sat

First opened by notorious playboy Rolf Eden in the late 1960s, Big Eden was long synonymous with the tacky, nouveau-riche scene in West Berlin. Except for the French GIs who were stationed in town, or teenage girls who didn't know any better, nobody would be caught dead here. Around the turn of the millennium, however, Big Eden was taken over by new management and transformed almost overnight into a slightly camp, very hip club. It was soon also nurturing an association with acts from trendy Berlin music labels such as Kitty-yo.

Nowadays, Big Eden is a fun place to come if you like dancing to R 'n' B, electroclash, house or disco. You can also catch live acts such as French actress-singer-songwriter Julie Delpy or synthpoppers Zoot Woman. There's just one, huge dance floor, surrounded by neon-lit booths for relaxing.

Rote Rosen *punky bar in rowdy area* `10 G2`
Adalbertstrasse 90, Kreuzberg
Open from 8pm nightly

This colourful bar in the seedy Kreuzberg 36 neighbourhood is regaining ground with bar-crawlers after a period out of favour. The name "red roses" derives from an alias of punk band Die Toten Hosen, which sometimes plays here. Not to be confused with Roses, a campy lesbian bar nearby.

Bierhimmel *gay/mixed favourite* `10 G2`
Oranienstrasse 183, Kreuzberg
Open from 2pm daily

By day, Bierhimmel ("beer heaven") is one of the most popular cafés in Kreuzberg 36. After the sun sets, as less coffee and more beer and cocktails are ordered, Bierhimmel eases into lounge bar mode. It attracts a predominantly gay crowd, but is very welcoming and relaxed with everybody.

Ankerklause *boisterous pub* `10 G4`
Kottbusser Damm 104, Kreuzberg • 030 69 35 64 9
\>> www.ankerklause.de
Open 10am -late Tue–Sun; club night Thu

Once a boat tours ticket office, this nautical-themed bar is loud, packed and trashy. The soundtrack is provided by a jukebox stocked with rockabilly, surf tunes, 60s beat, punk and indie music. In summer, the crowd spills onto the bank of the canal.

Madonna *bar caught in a time warp* `10 H3`
Wiener Strasse 22, Kreuzberg • 030 61 16 94 3
Open from 3pm daily

Like much of the neighbourhood, Madonna is still dominated by a black leather-clad crowd nearly 20 years after the bar opened. Only the addition of new beer brands and 250 whiskies to the bar list, and in the background some indie rock songs that have been released since 1988, mark the passage of time.

Watergate *stylish riverside club* `11 A4`
Falckensteinstrasse 49, Kreuzberg • 030 61 28 03 94
\>> www.water-gate.de Opening times vary; check website

A former commercial building with fabulous views over the Spree now exudes house, electro and techno grooves. Downstairs there is a spacious dance floor; above it is the Waterfloor Lounge. Both have high-tech video screens and minimalist furniture to complement the minimal electronic sounds.

Konrad Tönz *suave retro club* `11 A4`

Falckensteinstrasse 30, Kreuzberg • 030 61 23 25 2
>> www.konradtoenzbar.de Open from 8:15pm Tue–Sun

Named after the main character in a 1960s–70s detective show on German TV, Konrad Tönz heavily plays up the 70s look, with patterned wallpaper and beige and orange furniture. DJs spin nostalgic, trashy and freaky sounds from all over the world, including East German music from the 60s and 70s.

Haifischbar *classy cocktail bar* `9 D4`

Arndtstrasse 25, Kreuzberg • 030 69 11 35 2
>> www.haifischbar-berlin.de Open from 8pm nightly

This cocktail bar in Kreuzberg's more settled neighbourhood near Chamissoplatz attracts a hip, 30-ish crowd. There's a range of cocktails, beers and spirits, and some decent snacks, including sushi. Many patrons are happy to stay here all evening to chill out and chat (dancing is not really an option).

Wirtschaftswunder *timeless, cosy bar* `9 C4`

Yorckstrasse 81, Kreuzberg • 030 22 68 83 87
Open 5pm–5am daily (to 6am weekends)

Every night over two decades, Wirtschaftswunder's long cocktail list (the Caipirinha variations and shooters are especially good) and solid selection of light meals have attracted patrons and probably still will when other establishments have been and gone. Kidney-shaped tables and formica abound.

Gay Neighbourhoods

Berlin has always been home to one of Europe's largest homosexual communities, even when gays were persecuted by the Nazis and driven under-ground. Nowadays, gay and lesbian life is highly visible in four main neighbourhoods. The bars and clubs around **Motzstrasse** and **Nollendorfplatz** in Schöneberg (Map 8 H3, *see p130*) attract older, leather-clad men. In Kreuzberg, alternative or punk lesbians congregate at places near **Oranienstrasse** (Map 10 F2), while the more genteel **Mehringdamm** (Map 9 C4) draws a mixed lesbian and gay crowd. East of **Schönhauser Allee** in Prenzlauer Berg (Map 4 F1) is a mecca for lesbians and gays alike. If a rainbow flag is hanging outside a place, you know it's gay-operated or at least gay-friendly.

KitKat Club *decadent, pan-sexual club*
Bessemerstrasse 2–14, Schöneberg
⑤ Papestrasse or bus 204
≫ www.kitkatclub.de Opening times vary; check website

The name of this club is taken from the kinky nightclub in Christopher Isherwood's novella *I Am a Camera*, which is about bohemian goings-on in 1930s Berlin. That original, fictional KitKat Club where anything goes was made world famous in *Cabaret* – the 60s musical (and later film) that also inspired by Isherwood's stories.

This incarnation of the KitKat Club first opened in 1994, and quickly became the brand name for wild parties in Berlin. After various legal and illegal locations in Schöneberg (the district where Isherwood lived in the 30s; *see p130*) and Kreuzberg, the club settled in its current, legal home in 2000 – a former brewery building in an out-of-the-way neighbourhood in southern Schöneberg, near Tempelhof.

It's important to check the KitKat's website or Berlin club listings to make sure of the theme on a given night at the club. Ascertain whether the crowd is going to be straight, gay or mixed, and if you should be in fetish or bondage gear, leather, gold lamé or nothing at all. Lurkers are not welcome so, if you are summoning up the nerve to go, be prepared to dress the part and join in with the party, not just watch on the sidelines. Trance and new-age Goa sounds add to the mesmerizing, sexually charged atmosphere.

Parties in a similar vein can be found elsewhere in Berlin at the **Club Culture Houze** (Map 11 A4, Görlitzer Strasse 71, Kreuzberg, www.club-culture-houze.de), a multi-levelled theme park with dungeon rooms and other settings. The **Darkside** (Map 9 D4, Nostitzstr. 30, Kreuzberg, www.darkside-club.de) is for more upmarket patrons of all persuasions (not always on the same night). Again, check the respective websites to work out when you can do your thing.

Green Door *cocktail bar for hipsters* `8 H3`

Winterfeldtstrasse 50, Schöneberg • 030 21 52 51 5
>> www.greendoor.de Open 6pm–3am Mon–Sat, 8pm–3am Sun

Until recently, the Green Door stood out among the ragtag elements around Winterfeldtplatz. The area now has many classy joints, but the retro-style Green Door, in all its leather and patterned wallpaper chic, still beckons the discerning patron with its expertly mixed Screwdrivers, served by a coolly elegant staff.

Havanna *Afro-Cuban rhythms* `8 H5`

Hauptstrasse 30, Schöneberg • 030 78 48 56 5
>> www.havanna-berlin.de
Open from 9pm Wed, from 10pm Fri & Sat

The four dance floors of salsa, merengue, R 'n' B, disco reggae and soul at Havanna are always popular with gregarious expat Cubans and native Berliners alike. Come for an hour's instruction before the club opens if you want to hone your salsa moves.

Drinking Alfresco in Berlin

As soon as the winter snowstorms subside, Berliners like to come out into the open to enjoy their coffees and alcoholic beverages. Almost every café has tables out on the street from the time they open until 10pm, when activities are forced indoors by German law. For the most interesting streetlife scenes, sit outside at **Café Einstein** *(see p124)*, which stands on the prestigious Unter den Linden boulevard near Germany's centre of power, or try **Café Adler** (Map 9 D1, Friedrichstr. 206, Kreuzberg), which is located at Checkpoint Charlie *(see p14)*, the famous former East-West border crossing.

The beer garden is a German tradition dating from the late 19th century. **Prater** (Map 4 F1, Kastanienallee 7–9, Prenzlauer Berg) has one of the most popular beer gardens in Berlin, while **Kastanie** (Map 1 B5, Schloss Strasse 22, Charlottenburg), near the Schloss Charlottenburg,

is a bit off the beaten track but rewards those who make the trip with a garden, cheap beer and light meals. **Kaiserstein** (Map 9 c4, Mehringdamm 45), in the heart of the Kreuzberg 61 district, combines a beer garden with a restaurant serving fine international cuisine and well-mixed cocktails. High-powered types like to discuss deals over a beer and barbecue at **Café am Neuen See** in the Tiergarten *(see p134)*. If you're visiting Wannsee *(see p140)*, end the day with a beer at **Loretta am Wannsee** (at S-Bahn station Wannsee).

A newer phenomenon is beach bars, complete with reclining beach chairs, which are colonizing the Mitte and Friedrichshain shores of the Spree river. Best of these are the funky **YAAM** beach bar *(see p118)*, the **Strandbar** in Monbijou park in Mitte (Map 6 E2), and the posher **Bundespressestrand** (Map 5 A2, Kapelleufer/Reinhardtstrasse), across the river from the Tiergarten.

MS Hoppetosse *party boat* `11 B4`

Eichenstrasse 4, Treptow • 030 53 32 03 49 (info),
030 53 32 03 40 (reservations: recommended)
>> www.arena-berlin.de Open from noon Tue–Fri, from 2pm
Sat, from 11am Sun; sometimes closed for private parties

In the last few years, Berliners have been rediscovering their river as a place for refreshment during the day and for partying at night. Of various riverside developments sprouting up, the Arena at Treptow is the biggest *(see p96)*. This is where *MS Hoppetosse* is docked – a riverboat that has been transformed into a popular restaurant, bar and club. Have a drink in the gentle breeze on the upper deck of the boat, from where you can see sculptor Jonathan Borofsky's huge metal figures out on the water.

Hoppetosse's international menu – available day and night – includes salads, fish and vegetarian options (come from noon to 3pm for a good lunch deal). At night, clubbers rock the boat to reggae, salsa and electronic dance grooves.

Black Girls Coalition *wild parties* `11 C1`

Samariterstrasse 32, Friedrichshain • 0179 38 14 36 3
>> www.blackgirlscoalition.de Check website for party dates

Founded by drag queen Paisley Dalton in New York in the 1990s, this self-help group for African Americans later relocated to Berlin. As well as providing information about jobs, housing and immigration, BGC also throws gender- and genre-bending parties, mixing punk, electroclash and drag shows.

Panorama Bar/Berghain *techno club* `11 A2`

Am Wriezener Bahnhof, Friedrichshain
>> www.berghain.de Open from midnight Fri & Sat

A former power station in a remote, post-industrial, Friedrichshain neighbourhood now houses a dance floor and bar. The 10-minute walk from the train station doesn't deter the cognoscenti, who come for cutting-edge electronic sounds and visuals courtesy of the Ostgut crew. Gays and straights mingle happily.

K17 *the true home of the Berliner Goths* `11 D1`

Pettenkoferstrasse 17A, Friedrichshain • 030 42 08 93 00
>> www.k17.de Open from 9pm Tue–Sat

Located on the eastern fringe of Friedrichshain, K17's three dance floors have become shrines for black-clad youth, be they teased-hair Goths or long-tressed Death Metallers. Sounds range from morosely hypnotic Goth and its menacing cousin dark wave to deafening metal, electronic body music and industrial.

Matrix *diverse dance floors* `11 B3`
Warschauer Platz 18, Friedrichshain • 030 29 36 99/90
>> www.matrix-berlin.de
Open from 9pm Tue & Thu, from 10pm Wed, Fri & Sat

Large groups of revellers flock to this subterranean club, which has four dance floors catering to many tastes, including rock, techno and more mainstream dance-pop. Tuesday and Thursday nights feature a revival of the famous West Berlin Rock-It club with its musical diet of punk, indie, Goth and industrial. Wednesday is for "Ladies First", when female guests can enjoy free entrance before midnight. Friday Night Fever and Saturday's Disco Village are devoted to poppier or more electronic sounds.

In summer, the venue opens up its popular indoor pool and lounge area. After heating up on the dance floors, you can order a tropical drink and ice cream, and chill out in a beach chair here. Complete with people dressed as mermaids and beach boys, it's cheesy but fun: bring a skimpy swimming costume.

YAAM *ad-hoc club with Caribbean street vibe* `10 H1`
Stralauer Platz 35, Friedrichshain • 030 61 51 35 4
>> www.yaam.de Beach bar open from 6pm daily; market open 2–10pm Sun (club events from 10pm)

The "young and African art market", or YAAM, describes the origins of this unique Afro-Caribbean club, which is more of an urban playground than an organized venue. Originally set up on the Treptow shore of the Spree river, near the Arena *(see p96)*, YAAM has recently moved upriver and now occupies a beach-side lot near the Ostbahnhof train station. Every Sunday from afternoon until late in the evening, sound systems are set up, and the corner fills with Berliners young and old checking out the market stalls and "Kidz Corner". Games of streetball and hackysack take place, with reggae, dancehall or dub percolating from the background. Flagging energy levels are revived with Caipirinhas and Mojitos, and Caribbean snacks such as jerk chicken. YAAM also hosts the occasional techno and hiphop DJ.

Narva Lounge *groovy hangout* `11 B3`
Warschauer Platz 18, Friedrichshain • 030 29 36 99 91 3
>> www.narva-lounge.de Open from 10pm Fri & Sat

Located in a former electric light factory, Narva Lounge
has two dancefloors – serving house, garage and
other electronic, funky grooves – and a generous
lounge, with inviting sofas and a well-stocked bar.
It offers the now traditional Berlin experience of
dancing and hanging out in one location.

Schwarzsauer *popular meeting place* `4 F1`
Kastanienallee 13, Prenzlauer Berg • 030 44 85 63 3
Open 8am–6am daily, hot meals until 5pm, sushi after 7pm

There is no dearth of bars on trendy Kastanienallee,
but Schwarzsauer, by virtue of its longevity, is still the
best known. The 90s black and copper design has
aged well, and the affordable cocktails and drinks are
now complemented by sushi in the evenings. Come
here before a night at nearby Bastard *(see p97)*.

Gagarin *homage to a famous Russian* `4 G2`
Knaackstrasse 22, Prenzlauer Berg • 030 44 28 80 7
>> www.bar-gagarin.de Open 10am–2am daily

Soviet cosmonaut Yuri Gagarin – who became the first
human to travel in space when he orbited Earth in the
Vostok 1 rocket on 12 April 1961 – is the inspiration
for the striking decor at this hangout in the heart of
Prenzlauer Berg. The furniture looks as if it has been
taken straight from the set of a 60s sci-fi movie, and
portraits of the great man beam out from a backdrop
of fanciful planets and spaceships on the walls.

The menu is in a Russian vein too, with *pelmeni*
(Russian ravioli), blinis (savoury or sweet buckwheat
pancakes) and borsch (beetroot soup) providing the
foundation for Baltika beer and high-proof vodkas.
Gagarin's management also runs the **Pasternak**
restaurant next door *(see p45)*; the **Gorki Park** café
(Map 4 E2, Weinbergsweg 25, www.gorki-park.de),
and the **Potemkin** restaurant (Map 8 G3, Viktoria-
Luise-Platz 5, www.restaurant-potemkin.de).

Icon *subterranean breakbeats*

Cantianstrasse 15, Prenzlauer Berg
030 48 49 28 78 • ⑪ Eberswalder Strasse
≫ www.iconberlin.de Open usually from 11pm Fri & Sat
& for special events; check website for details

When it first opened in the mid-1990s, Icon was a welcome replacement for the defunct Toaster as Berlin's premier location for drum 'n' bass and other breakbeat-based music. Those styles still form the core of the subterranean club, with some reggae, ragga, hip-hop, old school techno, bigbeat, electro, 2step and downtempo added for good measure.

The club is set in a brick-built former brewery, accessed via a courtyard. There is one dance floor, several chillout areas and two bars offering unusually affordable beers and cocktails. The vibe is earthy and edgy, with a youngish crowd focused on dancing. Watch out for regular sets by top resident DJs, including Recycle and Ninja Tunes, and international visitors such as Metalheadz from the UK.

NBI *living-room electronics* **4 F1**

Schönhauser Allee 36, Prenzlauer Berg • 030 44 05 16 81
≫ www.neueberlinerinitiative.de
Open from 8pm nightly (acts start around 8 or 10pm)

An electronic music laboratory and lounge bar, the New Berlin Initiative, or NBI, has moved several times and is now located in the Kulturbrauerei cultural centre in Prenzlauer Berg *(see p131)*. The move to this posher location is not likely to dull NBI's reputation for cutting-edge sounds.

NBI hosts live acts from local German labels such as City Centre Offices, Raster-Noton or Gudrun Gut's Monika Enterprises. The premises are a hub of experimental music – NBI releases electronica on its own record label, including three critically acclaimed NBI compilations. Contrary to the popular image of electronic music as a cold, distant and inhuman genre, the NBI scene is warm and nurturing, which is reflected in the venue's subdued design – more living room than industrial.

Frannz Club *club with a long history* `4 F1`

Schönhauser Allee 36, Prenzlauer Berg
030 72 62 79 33 3 (info), 030 72 62 79 36 0 (restaurant)
≫ www.frannz.de Bar open noon–4am Mon–Fri,
10am–4am Sat & Sun; check website for club programme

First opened as a youth club in the GDR in 1970, the
Frannz Club has had a chequered history. Formerly
called the Franz Club (one "n"), it became a very
popular venue for live acts soon after the fall of the
Wall, but by the mid-90s it had fallen by the wayside.
After an almost decade-long hiatus and an unhappy
incarnation as a Bavarian beer hall, it has reopened
as the Frannz Club (double "n") in the Kulturbrauerei
complex *(see p131)*, set alongside various other live
music venues and clubs. It now includes a restaurant
(see p45) and attracts an older, more sophisticated
crowd. The kitchen is open all day and night, serving

up a range of international cuisine – pasta, meat, fish
and vegetarian dishes, and typical diner fare such
as burgers and chips – all washed down with beer.
There's a brunch buffet on Saturday and Sunday,
and a very popular beer garden in summer.

The club's main floor hosts live acts of various
stripes, including a weekly slot devoted to local
newcomers. Resident DJs regularly manage to fill the
floors with tunes in the establishment's preferred
musical styles of soul, dance classics, indie pop and
salsa. (There's salsa dance instruction on Monday
nights.) The relaxed, 30-plus patrons – often a mix of
straight and gay – are not afraid to show their
enthusiasm for tunes that may evoke fond youthful
memories or are simply highly danceable, whether
new or old. Much of the crowd comes for a full
night's worth of dancing and dining.

streetlife

A century ago, Berlin was created from about 20 small towns, still discernible in the city's varied neighbourhoods. Ku'damm and other elegant boulevards to the west have long attracted a wealthy crowd. To the east, Mitte is now Berlin's hottest district, attracting visitors from around the world. Outside the city centre, Kreuzberg, Prenzlauer Berg and Friedrichshain are other characterful districts with a burgeoning nightlife.

Streetlife

Unter den Linden and
Potsdamer Platz *rebuilt heart of Mitte*

5 C3

The soaring **Brandenburger Tor** (Berlin's 18th-century version of the Acropolis entrance in Athens) marks the start of Unter den Linden – the main thoroughfare in Mitte. The historic boulevard, originally a route to royal hunting grounds, was planted with lime trees in the 17th century, hence its name, "under the limes". Until it was bombed in World War II, Unter den Linden was famous for shopping and dining. The rebuilt boulevard has fewer shops and restaurants, but there are still many stately buildings, world-class museums, opera houses and theatres, and below the Brandenburger Tor, **Pariser Platz** is lined with embassies and corporate headquarters.

The Linden is at its best on Friday afternoons and Saturdays in summer, when Berliners stroll down the boulevard – a practice that has not changed over the centuries. Coffee shops near the Brandenburger Tor do a brisk trade, including the **Adlon** café *(see p148)*.

Heading eastward along Unter den Linden, you come to a few shops and cafés. The **Opernpalais** café and restaurant at No. 5 (www.opernpalais.de) serves delectable pastries and cakes. Further up the road, **Berlin-Story** at No. 40 *(see p51)* is a treasure trove of Berlin literature and souvenirs. You can lunch at a branch of **Café Einstein** at No. 42 *(see p135)* or **Lindenlife** (No. 44). A small **antiques market** (Saturday & Sunday) lies by the river next to the **Deutsches Historisches Museum** *(see p70)*.

South of the Brandenburger Tor are the shining high-rises of **Potsdamer Platz** (Map 5 A5), including the **Sony Center** (www.sonycenter.de), which houses the **Arsenal** cinema *(see p92)*. The only building on the square that predates World War II is **Weinhaus Huth**, which is now home to the DaimlerChrysler corporation and a restaurant (www.j-diekmann.de). In the evening, the old **Josty Bar** *(see p106)* and **Billy Wilder's** (www.billywilders.de) are good choices for champagnes and fruity cocktails.

For the very latest on Berlin go to ≫ www.realcity.dk.com

Scheunenviertel *hippest area of Mitte* `5 D1`

Long a run-down city quarter, almost forgotten in the shadow of East Germany's Fernsehturm *(see p72)*, Scheunenviertel became Berlin's hottest destination for the young and hip crowd immediately after the fall of the Wall in November 1989. Today, an odd mix of long-time residents, artists, students, yuppies, bankers and Russian Jews gives the district an exciting new face and lively nightlife. The bars and cafés on **Oranienburger Strasse** are thronged day and night, with people spilling out onto the pavements. The quieter side streets, such as **Auguststrasse** and **Sophienstrasse**, have an interesting mix of avant-garde galleries and antiques shops.

Named the Scheunenviertel – "barn quarter" – by the Nazis, the area was the city's main Jewish district until World War II, during which the original inhabitants were transported to concentration camps. Jewish life has returned, however. The **Neue Synagoge** *(see p73)*, first built in 1866, has been revived as a cultural centre, and the district's grey and red tenement houses have been restored. Kosher food is available at places like **Café Orange** (Oranienburger Strasse 32) and the **Beth Café** (Tucholskystr. 60).

At Oranienburger Strasse 54–6, the huge 19th-century **Tacheles**, originally a shopping mall, is now an arts centre with a café and club (www.tacheles.de). The area contains many other 19th-century buildings, most of them former warehouses that have been converted into offices, shops, restaurants and cinemas. Best of all is the **Hackesche Höfe** complex (Map 6 E1), which incorporates a series of Art Nouveau courtyards. Here you will find many upmarket boutiques *(see pp52–3)*, the **Hackescher Hof** restaurant *(see p31)* and the **Chamäleon** variety theatre (Rosenthaler Strasse 40–41, www.chamaeleon-variete.de). A good place for East German souvenirs is the **Ampelmann Galerie** (Hof 5, www.ampelmann.de).

Friedrichstrasse *elegant shops* `5 C4`

Until the 1940s, Friedrichstrasse was one of Berlin's most important shopping boulevards, bisected by Unter den Linden into fancy southern and rougher northern halves. The bombs of World War II and subsequent neglect under the Socialists marked the end of that era. Nowadays, contemporary buildings by Jean Nouvel, O M Ungers and I M Pei have transformed the southern part of the road, where upmarket shops are clustered at the **Friedrichstadtpassagen** and around **Galeries Lafayette** *(see p50)*. These attract a youngish, international crowd.

The side-streets contain beautiful historic buildings and some fine restaurants, including **Borchardt** *(see p28)* and **Lutter & Wegner** *(p29)*, and nice little coffee houses such as **Café Möhring** (Charlottenstrasse 55), which was founded in 1898. In winter, the Christmas market on neighbouring **Gendarmenmarkt** *(Map 5 D4; see pp18–19)* offers an enticing mix of food stalls, crafts, joyful carol singing and entertainments.

Savignyplatz *bohemian spot* `8 E1`

This charming square and surrounding roads have long been an arty quarter, where you could easily spend a whole day browsing through galleries, antiques shops and bookshops such as **Bücherbogen** *(see p60)*. The square itself is a pleasant place to relax, with its tree-lined paths and benches set around a quaint statue of a boy trying to control his goats. For refreshment, **Café Savigny** (Grolmanstr. 53) specializes in traditional German fruitcakes and tarts.

Savignyplatz is always busy with diners on summer evenings. Restaurants on or just off the square include **Florian** and **Mar y Sol** *(see p40 for both)*, the Italian **Brunello** (Knesebeckstrasse 18) and **Lubitsch** (Bleibtreustrasse 47), which has an international menu with many organic ingredients. Further restaurants and shops can be found in two passages: one following the S-Bahn arcades between Bleibtreustrasse and Savignyplatz; the other running between Knesebeckstrasse and Uhlandstrasse.

Kurfürstendamm and Tauentzienstrasse *grand avenues*

8 F2

In the heart of Charlottenburg, these two boulevards intersect at **Breitscheidplatz**, in front of the landmark **Kaiser-Wilhelm-Gedächtnis-kirche** *(see p79)* and the adjacent **Europa-Center** (www.europa-center-berlin.de). The latter is a 1960s-built mall with a good grocery store, ice-cream parlour and the Thermen spa *(see p135)*. However, the main action is around the huge fountain on Breitscheidplatz. In summer, cool your feet in the water while watching the street performers and Vietnamese portrait painters at work in the square.

Walking eastward brings you onto **Tauentzienstrasse**, which is dominated by flagships, such as for **Adidas** (No. 15; www.adidas.com) and **Nike** (No. 7; www.nike.com), and the department store **Peek & Cloppenburg** (No. 19; www.peekundcloppenburg.de). The landmark building at the end of the boulevard is the Kaufhaus des Westens, or **KaDeWe** *(see p63)* emporium, which has a wonderful gourmet food hall on its 6th floor.

An alternative to the KaDeWe food counters are the many *Imbisse* (food stalls) found on **Wittenbergplatz** (Map 8 G2); one of the best is the **Neuland Imbiss**, where you should order a spicy *Currywurst (see p36)*. On Saturdays, the square comes alive with a market selling flowers, farm foods and health products.

Leading west from Breitscheidplatz, **Kurfürstendamm** (otherwise known as **Ku'damm**) was built in the 1880s. It is lined with a mixture of elegant city mansions and international chain stores. Look out for the angular glass and steel **Neues Kranzler Eck** office building by Helmut Jahn on the corner of Joachims-thaler, which is a good example of Berlin's exciting new architecture. Further along are some German and French restaurants, but the coffee houses, such as **Café Carras** or **Café Balzac**, are more inviting.

The neighbourhood becomes quieter and more elegant the further west you walk down Ku'damm, where you'll find expensive shops such as **Jil Sander** *(see p58)* and the **Porsche Design Store** *(see p59)*.

Streetlife

Fasanenstrasse *attractive side-street* `8 E2`

A tree-lined avenue leading off both north and south from Kurfürstendamm *(see p127)*, Fasanenstrasse is one of Berlin's most pleasant roads. At its northern end, the boutique **Savoy Hotel Berlin** and first-class **Kempinski Bristol** *(see p154 for both)* exude an Old-World atmosphere rarely found elsewhere in Berlin today. Both hotels have good restaurants and bars.

Opposite the Kempinski is the **Jewish Synagogue and Community Centre** – a 1950s building that incorporates elements of the original, Romanesque-style synagogue that was built in 1912 – and the beautifully curving windows of private banking house **Löbbecke**. On the other side of Ku'damm are some small boutiques such as **Röckl Handschuhe** (www.roeckl.de), which sells stylish gloves and accessories, and Berlin's leading auction house, **Villa Grisebach** (www.villa-grisebach.de), which holds regular sales of paintings, sculptures and photography from the 19th and 20th centuries. Inviting neighbourhood restaurants include the **Via Condotti** with its traditional Italian menu (Fasanenstrasse 73; www.viacondotti-berlin.de).

The area's main draw, though, is the **Literaturhaus Berlin** (Fasanenstrasse 23; www.literaturhaus-berlin.de) – the haunt of many leading writers. It has a programme of readings and discussions, and houses a superb bookstore, **Kohlhaas & Company**, as well as the **Wintergarten Café**, where you can treat yourself to traditional German strawberry cake and whipped cream in lovely formal gardens.

Schlesische Strasse *funky outpost* `11 A4`

Centred around the metro station of Schlesisches Tor, and hemmed in by the Spree river and Landwehrkanal, this corner of Berlin is a wild mix of run-down houses, Turkish shops, street cafés and quirky bars. Join the laid-back inhabitants at bars such as **Heinz Minki** (Schlesisches Tor 3) or enjoy performing arts at **Galerie Tristesse** (No. 38) and club nights at other hip spots such as **Watergate** *(see p111)*.

For the very latest on Berlin go to ➤➤ www.realcity.dk.com

Kreuzberg *Berlin's alternative centre* `10 F2`

The district of Kreuzberg, which lies to the south of the reunified city centre and was formerly part of West Berlin bordering the East, has found a new status as the city's most fascinating and culturally diverse district. It is a hive of activity day and night.

Kreuzberg has long been divided into the working-class area called **SO 36** and a larger, more bourgeois quarter called **61** (named after the old postcodes). Start with 61 at **Checkpoint Charlie** *(see p14)*, which from 1961 to 1989 was the only crossing-point between East and West Berlin. Here, the small and cheeky Leftist newspaper *Taz* has its headquarters, next door to the **Sale e Tabbachi** restaurant *(see p42)*. Remains of the Wall can be seen just a few minutes' walk to the west, behind the **Martin-Gropius-Bau** *(see p83)*. The latter is a glorious, late 19th-century exhibition hall with a nice gallery café and outdoor

seating in summer. Also nearby are the ruins of the **Anhalter Bahnhof** (Map 9 C2), a grand station built in the 1880s, and **Tempodrom** (Möckernstrasse 10; www.tempodrom.de), which is a music venue set inside a large tent-like structure.

To the east, SO 36 is a rougher area, with graffiti-smeared houses. **Kottbusser Tor** (Map 10 G3), an ugly 1970s square, has a small daily fruit market, but the real shopping is done along busy **Oranienstrasse**, which is crowded with cafés, bars and unusual shops, such as **DIM** *(see p64)*. Don't leave without having sampled authentic Turkish food at **Hasir** *(see p41)*.

The lovely **Paul-Lincke-Ufer** along the **Landwehr-kanal** is one of the nicest parts of Kreuzberg. This stretch of restored, 19th-century mansions is home to lively pubs and **Café am Ufer** (No. 42–3). On the opposite bank is the **Türkischer Markt** *(see p62)*, where you can sample Middle Eastern food.

>> *Kreuzberg is home to the world's largest Turkish community outside of Turkey*

Streetlife

Schöneberg *bohemian area turning hip* 8 H3

Before World War II, Schöneberg was a red-light and gay district, and it remains a colourful neighbourhood. Gentrification is fast taking place in the area around **Winterfeldtplatz** and **Nollendorfplatz**. The Saturday market on Winterfeldtplatz is great for flower stalls, vintage records and some of Berlin's best bagels and cinnamon rolls. **Eisenacherstrasse** and **Nollendorf-strasse** are home to many antiques dealers. You can kick back in the chairs in front of **Café M** (Goltzstr. 33), wiggle your toes in the sand at the **Slumberland** pub (Goltzstr. 24) or sip a cocktail at the **Green Door** (Winterfeldtstr. 50; www.greendoor.de).

    Motzstrasse is the epicentre of Berlin's large gay community and has many gay bars. A memorial at the Nollendorfplatz S-Bahn station commemorates the homosexuals killed during the Third Reich; another remembers the gay Anglo-American writer Christopher Isherwood, whose fictional *Berlin Stories*, published in 1946, were based on his time here in the 1930s.

Friedrichshain *up-and-coming quarter* 11 C1

One of Berlin's hottest areas is an intriguing blend of derelict buildings, cheap studios, avant-garde galleries and buzzing bars and clubs *(see pp117–19)*. The main boulevard, **Karl-Marx-Allee**, which becomes **Frankfurter Allee** further east, is lined with relics of 1950s Stalinist architecture – the grand but lifeless façades of which are slowly being revived. On **Strausberger Platz, Haus Berlin** and **Noiquattro** *(see p44 for both)* are contrasting examples of the restaurant scene. More nightlife can be found around **Boxhagener Platz** (Map 11 C2), where all-night bars like **Goldfisch** (Grünbergerstr. 67) and **Himmelreich** (Simon-Dach-Str. 36) are among the hip spots.

    Perhaps the strongest defining feature of Friedrichshain is its large remnant of the Berlin Wall of 1961–89. This stretches along Mühlenstrasse in front of the river (Map 11 A3) and has been painted by more than 100 artists from around the world: it is referred to as the **East Side Gallery** (www.eastsidegallery.com).

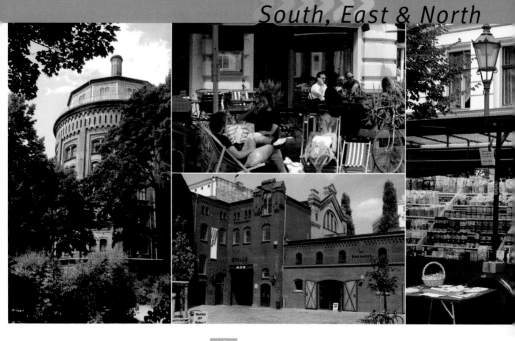

Prenzlauer Berg *lively neighbourhood* `4 G1`

In Socialist days, this northeastern district of Berlin was home to many dissident writers and artists who spoke out against the regime, giving Prenzlauer Berg an enduring association with alternative culture. Today, "Prenzlberg", as it is often called, is less cutting-edge but has a reputation as one of the city's best districts for nightlife.

Kollwitzplatz is the noisy and turbulent heart of Prenzlauer Berg, with numerous bars lining the square and roads nearby, in particular **Knaackstrasse**, **Kollwitzstrasse** and **Wörther Strasse**. Among some excellent restaurants are **Gugelhof** *(see p44)* and **Drei** *(see p45)*; for fish and game dishes, try **Zander** (Kollwitzstrasse 50). The Russian bar and restaurant **Pasternak** *(see p45)* is especially popular and helps to turn the neighbourhood into a big party zone in summer. To the north of Kollwitzplatz, **Husemann-strasse** is a pristine, restored 19th-century street – No. 1 is the location of one of the area's oldest bars, **Restauration 1900** (www.restauration-1900.de).

A market on Kollwitzplatz sells fresh produce from neighbouring Brandenburg: come on Thursday for the **Ökomarkt** (noon–7) if you like health foods and organic produce. However, if you prefer more hearty German food and alcohol, head towards the landmark **Wasserturm** (water tower; Map 4 G2), which stands on a low hill by Knaackstrasse, around which you will find more bars and restaurants.

Schönhauser Allee, the main shopping street in Prenzlauer Berg, has a wealth of second-hand and antiques shops. Head north along this road to reach the **Kulturbrauerei** complex (Map 4 F1; www. kulturbrauerei-berlin.de). Formerly a brewery, these huge yellow- and red-brick buildings now house the **Frannz** restaurant *(see p45)*, a club, cinema, theatre and shops. There are dance performances, live music and festivals here throughout the year. Just a few steps away, off Kastanienallee, is the **Prater** (www.pratergarten.de), which has one of Berlin's nicest beer gardens and is also the location of the quirky music venue **Bastard** *(see p96)*.

>> *For more about Berlin's street markets*, see p62

havens

Berlin is one of Europe's greenest capitals. A large area at the centre of the city is taken up by the Tiergarten park, and half of Greater Berlin is composed of natural forests and wetlands. Not to be missed are the Botanischer Garten and the vast landscaped parks of historical Potsdam, all within easy reach of the city centre. Berlin's Turkish and Russian baths are other good places to get away from hectic urban life.

Tiergarten *Berlin's green lung* `3 A5`

Berlin's famous park is located at the heart of the city and is accessible from various points, including the **Brandenburger Tor** *(see p13)* and **Potsdamer Platz** *(p124)* in the east. The **Zoologischer Garten** *(see p15)*, one of Europe's most popular zoos, takes up the southwest corner of the park.

Originally a royal hunting ground, in the 19th century it was landscaped by Peter Joseph Lenné, who laid it out in a fashionable English style with lawns and flowerbeds, and many lakes and canals.

When you walk beneath the Tiergarten's majestic trees and across the luxuriant green lawns, it is hard to imagine that immediately after World War II all the old trees in the park were chopped down for firewood, and potatoes were grown here to feed a desperate population. The replanted park includes elaborate flower gardens, such as the **Rhododendrongarten**. This lies close to the **Strasse des 17. Juni**, an avenue that divides the park into northern and southern parts.

The park is popular with families, who come to picnic and play games, and the pathways are always busy with cyclists, joggers and Nordic walkers (the ones striding along with poles). During summer weekends, Berlin's Turkish community throws huge barbecue parties near the Neo-Classical presidential palace, **Schloss Bellevue** (not open to the public), while one of the lawns in the middle of the park has become a popular meeting place for the city's gay community. In the northern section, the **Haus der Kulturen der Welt** *(see p75)* is a major venue for world music.

One of the best ways to enjoy the Tiergarten is to rent a rowing boat and explore its many waterways. Boats can be hired by the hour at **Café am Neuen See** (Map 8 G1, Lichtensteinallee 2, open daily). Another café, **Konditorei Buchwald** (Map 2 G4, Bartningallee 29, open daily) is famous for its chocolate biscuits and pear-and-cream cakes. The Spree river forms the northern boundary of the park, where you can catch a riverboat *(see box)*.

Café Einstein classic coffeehouse

Kurfürstenstrasse 58, Tiergarten • 030 26 15 09 6

>> www.cafeeinstein.com Open 9am–1am daily

An old favourite among Berlin's literati, Café Einstein is famous for its Viennese dishes, club sandwiches and excellent coffee. This is the original Einstein, housed in a villa with a lovely garden; there's another branch in Mitte *(see p124)*. Settle down with the free newspapers and be charmed by the friendly service.

Thermen am Europa-Center `8 F2`

Nürnberger Strasse 7, Charlottenburg • 030 25 75 76 0

>> www.thermen-berlin.de

Open 10am–midnight Mon–Sat, 10am–9pm Sun

Set in a 1960s tower, overlooking the rooftops of Charlottenburg, this spa offers indoor and open-air swimming pools in lush surroundings. Try the Roman-style baths (hot, warm and cold). Saunas and a massage are also included in the entrance fee. **Adm**

Würgeengel Kreuzberg life at its best

Dresdener Strasse 122, Kreuzberg • 030 61 55 56 0

>> www.wuergeengel.de Open from 7pm

Named after a Luis Buñuel film of 1962 (in English, *The Exterminating Angel*), this relaxing bar is a good example of Kreuzberg's culturally mixed scene. Perfect cocktails and Mediterranean dishes are served in a room that feels like a 1950s Latin American club lounge. Come here after a film at Babylon *(see p95)*.

Berlin by Boat

Several major waterways flow through Berlin: the Spree river cuts through the city centre; the Havel will take you to Potsdam and beyond; and the Landwehrkanal is the longest of several canals. Some of the main piers for boat trips are Burgstrasse (Map 6 E2), Moltkebrücke (Map 3 B4) and Haus der Kulturen der Welt (Map 3 A4). Operators include Reederei Riedel (030 69 34 64 6, www.reedereiriedel.de), which offers city tours and trips to Potsdam, with well-informed guides (ask for information in English, if required). A similar operator is **Stern und Kreis** (030 53 63 60 0, www.sternundkreis.de). **City Schiffahrt** (030 34 57 78 3, www.cityschiffahrt.de) includes more obscure parts of Berlin on its itineraries.

Havens

Sultan Hamam `9 A3`
Turkish delights

Bülowstrasse 57, Schöneberg • 030 21 75 33 75
» www.sultan-hamam.de Open noon–11pm daily;
men-only Mon; women-only Tue–Sat; families Sun

Over 200,000 Turks live in Berlin, so it is not surprising that the city has an excellent bath-house, offering a traditional Turkish steam bath alongside contemporary bio-saunas and light therapy. Women are given extra pampering with scrubs, pedicures and massages. **Adm**

Café am Engelbecken `10 G1`
tranquil retreat

Michaelkirchplatz am Engelbecken, Mitte • 030 28 37 68 16
» www.cafe-am-engelbecken.de Open from 10am daily

In the shadow of a bombed-out church that was once part of the no-man's-land near the Wall is a lovely café overlooking the waterway at the Luisenstädtischer Kanal *(see above)*. This is the place to enjoy a fancy cocktail and savour an optimistic, post-Cold-War atmosphere that can only be experienced in Berlin.

Luisenstädtischer Kanal `10 G1`
restored park

This formal park was first created in 1926 on the site of a mostly filled-in canal on the border of Mitte and Kreuzberg, which later became the border of East and West Berlin. The park was destroyed in the Cold War, but recent landscaping has restored the avenues and fountains to their former glory. A remnant of the original waterway has also been kept, to the benefit of nesting birds in spring and ice-skaters in winter.

Treptower Park `11 C5`
riverside stroll

Originally constructed in 1860 as a recreation area for Berlin's working class, this park by the Spree river still has the beer gardens and dance pavilions that were typical of German parks at the end of the 19th century. As in the old days, the dancing starts early in the afternoons at the weekend and is accompanied by enthusiastic consumption of beer, sausages and pickled cucumbers. Join in with the former East Berliners for a polka and other folk songs and dances.

Most of Treptower Park consists of grassy expanses surrounded by trees and hedges, which make the place perfect for sunbathing, a picnic or reading a book. It's impossible to miss the **Sowjetisches Ehrenmal**, a colossal memorial complex built to honour the 300,000 Red Army soldiers killed during the battle of Berlin in 1945. The park also contains the **Archenhold Sternwarte** (www.astw.de), a planetarium that boasts the world's longest refracting telescope (tours at 8pm Thu, 3pm Sat & Sun).

Arena Badeschiff *bathing revival*

`11 B4`

Eichenstrasse 4, Treptow • 030 53 32 03 0
» www.badeschiff.de Open May–Nov: 8am–midnight daily;
Dec–Apr: 10am–midnight daily

Berlin once had many "bathing ships" on the Spree.
Pollution and politics led to their disappearance, but
Arena Badeschif f marks a revival. Now one of Berlin's
coolest meeting points, it has on board a large
illuminated pool, sun decks, a bar and café. **Adm**

Die Banja *how to unwind like a Russian*

Leydenallee 79, Dahlem • 0172 30 00 08 0 • ⑤ Dahlem-Dorf
Open daily: reservations only

This Russian spa offers not only steam baths
and pools, but also massages, peeling and a good
whipping with birch twigs. Book in advance for
a small group (two to eight people) to enjoy an all-
encompassing experience of Russian bathing culture
and traditional food and drink. **Adm**

Botanischer Garten *floral journey*

Königin-Luise-Strasse 6–8, Dahlem
030 83 85 01 00 • ⑤ Dahlem-Dorf
» www.bottanischergartenberlin.de Open 9am–dusk Mon–Sat

This magnificent garden was created in the late 19th
century and is one of the world's largest botanical
gardens, covering 32 ha (about 80 acres). The
specimen trees, shrubs and herbaceous plants
are arranged according to their place of origin: you
can take a stroll from the biomes of the Americas,
through Europe and over to Asia. One of the most
spectacular features is a huge greenhouse built by
Alfred Koerner in 1906. This was inspired by Joseph
Paxton's famous Crystal Palace, built for the Great
Exhibition of 1851 in London, which no longer exists.
Koerner's version houses tropical plants, cacti,
medicinal plants and carnivorous plants.

The garden's Unter den Eichen restaurant has a
menu of German and international dishes. There is
also a shop where you can buy exotic seeds. **Adm**

Havens

Schlachtensee *nature reserve*
Ⓢ Berlin-Schlachtensee • Bootsverlei: Marinesteig 6A
Open in fine weather only; roughly 10am to sunset in summer
Die Fischerhütte: Fischerhüttenstrasse 136 • 030 36 75 26 34
Beer garden open 9am–10pm; restaurant open noon–midnight

The crystal-clear waters of the Schlachtensee
are the centrepiece of a nature reserve that lies
southwest of Berlin, halfway between the city and
Potsdam. Motorboats are not allowed on the lake,
which makes it idyllic for swimmers, canoeists
and fishing enthusiasts. The water often freezes in
winter, making it a popular destination for ice-skating
Berliners. Rowing boats can be rented at **Bootsverleih
am Schlachtensee**, while the hilly, northern side of
the lake offers great walks and views.

The best place for refreshments is **Die Fischerhütte**,
to the west of the lake, which was a public house
even in the days of Frederick the Great (1740–86).
It has a large Bavarian-style beer garden and a
restaurant run by Lutter & Wegner *(see p29)*.

Wannsee *royal pleasure ground*
Ⓢ Wannsee (33 km/21 miles southwest of Berlin)
Pfaueninsel ferry every 10 minutes from 10am to dusk

An affluent district by the Havel river, Wannsee has
many landscaped parks, including the 19th-century
royal pleasure ground of **Pfaueninsel** – a UNESCO
World Heritage Site. Set on an island in the river, this
contains spectacular follies built in the forms of
palaces and ancient Greek temples.

On the southern bank of the Havel, the 19th-century
Church of Saints Peter and Paul is an unusual mix of
Russian and Italian styles. It stands close to the
Blockhaus Nikolskoe, a Russian *dacha*, or wooden
house, that has been converted into a restaurant
(Nikolskoer Weg 15, 030 80 52 91 4).

Half-an-hour's walk southwest along the river is the
park of **Klein-Glienicke**. Here, you'll find a lodge
designed in a pseudo-Byzantine style and an alpine
landscape with hunting cabins. The **Klein-Glienicke
Palace** houses an excellent restaurant *(see p43)*.

Grunewald *beautiful area of forest*

🟢 Grunewald • Jagdschloss Grunewald: Hüttenweg 100
030 81 33 59 7 Open May–Oct: 10–5 Tue–Sun
Forsthaus Paulsborn: Hüttenweg 90 • 030 81 81 91 0
» www.forsthaus-paulsborn.de Open 11am–11pm Tue–Sun

What was once the royal hunting ground of Prussian kings and German emperors is now one of the foremost recreation areas of Berlin, with 35 sq km (14 sq miles) of lakes and forests.

The AVUS Autobahn (the world's first motorway, built in 1921) divides the park into two sections, each with its own character. To the east is the idyllic lake **Grunewaldsee** and surrounding forests of fir, birch and oak, where many Berliners come to exercise their dogs off the leash. The pretty Baroque hunting palace of **Jagdschloss Grunewald**, located at the southern end of the lake, has been transformed into a concert venue and art gallery, and contains paintings by old masters such as Cranach, Rubens and Van Dyck, as well as a collection of antique hunting weapons.

Close by is the old **Forsthaus Paulsborn** restaurant (see p43), which is good for venison, wild boar and other traditional German dishes.

West of the AVUS is a huge tract of hilly woodland, stretching as far as the river Havel. Crisscrossed by paths, this is a perfect area for walks and mountain-biking. At path intersections, follow the directions on the stone pillars to find the little **Teufelsee** ("Devil's lake"), where the popular German pastime of nude swimming is permitted.

For refreshments, make your way to the **Grunewald-turm** (Havelchaussee 61, www.grunewaldturm.de), an imposing tower built in 1889. At its foot is a café offering pastries and light meals, while the top offers a splendid view over the forest and river. Inline skaters (rollerbladers) can reach the tower on a special path running from S-Bahn Grunewald. From the tower, you have the option either to retrace your steps to S-Bahn Grunewald or catch bus 218 to S-Bahn Halensee (Map 7 A3), at the end of Ku'damm.

Potsdam *historic city*

🅢 Potsdam Hauptbahnhof (Line 1 from Friedrichstrasse)
» www.potsdam.de

The charming city of Potsdam is a 20-minute train journey southwest of Berlin. This old seat of the Prussian kings and modern capital of the State of Brandenburg has many splendid parks and sights, most of which can be visited on foot or by tram.

Potsdam's vast, famous **Park Sanssouci** ("park without cares") was constructed in the 18th century for Frederick the Great and contains many historic buildings, including the Rococo palace of **Schloss Sanssouci** (open 9–5 Tue–Sun, to 4pm Nov–Mar). Built by Frederick's favourite architect, Georg Wenzeslaus von Knobelsdorff, the palace stands dramatically at the top of a series of six terraces, which are adorned with vines, fig trees and fountains. Nearby is the surprisingly simple tomb of the king and his two favourite dogs.

The park – which is designated a UNESCO World Heritage Site – is divided into sections with different buildings. These include an exquisite, powder-blue Chinese tea house dating from 1756, Roman baths designed by Karl Friedrich Schinkel in 1829, and a Neo-Classical Orangery, built 1851–60 by Friedrich August Stüler. The Friedenskirche, built in 1845, was based on the San Clemente church in Rome.

Northeast of the modern city centre, beside the **Heiliger See** ("holy lake"), is another lovely park, **Neuer Garten**, designed by Peter Joseph Lenné in 1816. This is the perfect place for picnicking, and for swimming in the crystal-clear waters of the Heiliger See.

Overlooking the lake are the **Marmorpalais**, a Neo-Classical building with a marble façade (open 10–5 Tue–Sun, 10–4 Sat & Sun Nov–Mar), and the **Schloss Cecilienhof**, which was the setting of the historic Potsdam Conference of 1945. There is a German restaurant and characterful hotel at the Cecilienhof *(see p157)*. Also by the lake are the villas of Berlin's glitterati (their prevalence here is due in part to the local taxes, which are lower than in Berlin).

Potsdam's **Holländisches Viertel** ("Dutch Quarter") lies to the east of Park Sanssouci. Built in the mid-18th century to house traders from the Low Countries, the typically Netherlandish red-brick, gabled buildings now contain antiques shops, coffee houses and bars. Potsdam is not particularly known for its restaurants, but two good ones are the **Speckers zur Ratswaage**

(Am Neuen Markt 10, 0331 28 04 31 1), for its traditional Prussian interior and excellent international cuisine, and the **Villa Kellermann** (Mangerstrasse 34–6, 0331 29 15 72), which focuses on Mediterranean cooking and has a splendid view over the Heiliger See and Neuer Garten.

South of the station is the **Telegraphenberg** hill, which you can walk up to reach a leafy campus. Here, among several academic buildings that are acclaimed for their modern architecture, is one of Potsdam's most celebrated edifices: a solar observatory called the **Einsteinturm** (0331 29 17 41, guided tours by appointment only). This curvaceous tower of 1921 was built in an Expressionist-Modernist style by one of the pioneers of 20th-century architecture, Erich Mendelsohn, as a tribute to his friend Albert Einstein.

hotels

Berlin's hotels range from historic boarding houses, arty hostels and private apartments to boutique hotels and five-star resorts. The central districts of Mitte and Charlottenburg have the greatest choice of accommodation, but you'll find characterful places to stay in many other parts of Berlin. And thanks to fierce competition among the new hotels, the cost of a room in this city is now quite low.

HOTELS

There are constant changes in Berlin's hotel market and that seems to shake up the scene every two or three years. Berlin has recently gained many new five-star and designer hotels, which have joined an already impressive number of luxury accommodation options in the city. An equally welcome addition has been the clutch of tiny boutique hotels that have sprung up in former industrial buildings, in the 19th-century tenement houses of Kreuzberg and around quaint courtyards in Mitte.

Jürgen Scheunemann

German Luxury

For a taste of old-school German hospitality and luxury, book a night at the **Adlon Kempinski** *(see p148)*, the grand old lady of Berlin's hotels. The **InterContinental** *(see p151)* is a huge five-star modern classic with great views, while the **Kempinski Bristol Berlin** *(see p154)* in the heart off Ku'damm epitomizes the charm of western Berlin.

Ultra-Modern

Minimalist **Hotel Q!** *(see p155)* is a cool statement of futuristic urban accommodation. Cutting-edge style is also guaranteed at the **Ku'damm 101** *(see p155)*, another leading designer hotel, popular with the buzzing media and Internet crowd. The sleek **Radisson SAS** *(see p150)*, built around a vast aquarium, offers a bright, Scandinavian look.

Spas and Pools

The **Dorint Schweizerhof** *(see p153)*, a four-star hotel with revamped Bauhaus-style elements, has a great indoor pool and wellness area. For supreme indulgence, book a day at **Grand Hyatt's** *(see p150)* Olympus wellness club or relax at the high-tech oasis of the **Ku'damm 101** *(see p155)* – complete with steam bath and shiatsu treatment.

choice stays

Boutique Hotels

Two of Berlin's most charming boutique hotels, the **Dorint-Sofitel am Gendarmenmarkt** and the **Hotel Gendarm** *(see p149 for both)* offer understated yet sophisticated service in a cosy, elegant setting off historic Gendarmenmarkt. The **Savoy Hotel Berlin** *(see p154)*, dating back to 1929, is western Berlin's showcase hotel for old-style charm.

Art Hotels

Berlin offers an incredibly wide choice of eccentric "art hotels", such as **Propeller Island City Lodge** *(see p156)*, where each bizarre room is a work of art. At **Künstlerheim Luise** *(see p152)* you can choose from 50 different rooms, each created by a contemporary artist, and **MitArt Hotel** *(see p149)* is another hotel-gallery, with many paintings.

Bargains

For a great deal of affordable charm, stay a night at the 19th-century **Honigmond Hotel** *(see p151)*. Die-hard backpackers will prefer the **AO Hostel Berlin Zoo** *(see p156)*, as it is international, young, trendy and centrally located. Less expensive but more charming is **Transit** *(see p157)*, a Kreuzberg dorm-style – but hip – hotel.

Adlon Kempinski *the grand old lady* `5 B4`

Unter den Linden 77, Mitte • 030 22 61 0
>> www.hotel-adlon.de

Standing proudly opposite the Brandenburger Tor, the Adlon is the epitome of old-fashioned German hospitality. It first opened in 1907 as a state-of-the-art hotel – with elevators, electricity in all rooms, hot water and modern bathrooms – and soon became the living room of that era's noble families. Emperor Wilhelm II famously had a preference for the Adlon's suites over his nearby palace. After World War I, it evolved into a jet-set hotspot. Marlene Dietrich was discovered here, and Billy Wilder worked as a society dancer at the Sunday afternoon teas, while guests in the 1920s and 30s included Charlie Chaplin, Albert Einstein and the Rockefellers.

That first Adlon was largely destroyed in World War II, and the remains demolished in 1984. With the fall of the Wall, however, came resurrection. In 1997 the new Adlon was opened, and it is now a luxury Kempinski-chain hotel replicating much of the Neo-Classical decor of the old. Once again, Berlin's "grande dame" is the meeting point of the rich and powerful, its (bullet- and missile-proof) Presidential Suite the accommodation of choice for world leaders and Hollywood stars.

Beneath a stained-glass ceiling, the lobby of the Adlon is a lovely place in which to relax, with an exceptional bar and spacious sitting areas. Even if you're not a guest, it's worth coming here for a snack or a drink. A pianist sets the tone with romantic or jazzy tunes while guests are served with delicate sandwiches. The cocktail list is impressively long.

The Adlon's Junior Suites and Superior Deluxes overlook Unter den Linden and have marble bathrooms and top-class communication facilities. The price of one of these suites is surprisingly modest in comparison with those in five-star grand hotels in most other major world cities. **Expensive**

Dorint-Sofitel am Gendarmenmarkt *cosy boutique hotel*

`5 D4`

Charlottenstrasse 50–52, Mitte • 030 20 37 50
>> www.sofitel.com; www.aigner-gendarmenmarkt.de

Located just off the 17th-century Gendarmenmarkt square, this charming boutique hotel is run by Tini Countess Rothkirch, one of Berlin's best-known society hostesses, who prides herself on making guests feel welcome. The building was constructed during East Germany's Socialist days but has been transformed by the Swiss interior architects Klein and Haller into a place of contemporary, uncluttered style. Rooms are fairly spacious, and some offer a view of the adjacent French cathedral.

The hotel's famous restaurant, Aigner, is authentically Austrian – even the bentwood café furniture and wall fittings were transported here in the 1990s from the original Aigner restaurant in Vienna. On the menu are expertly prepared Austrian soups and meat dishes. **Expensive**

Art'otel Berlin Mitte *arty rooms*

`6 G4`

Wallstrasse 70–73, Mitte • 030 24 06 20
>> www.artotel.de

A contemporary hotel converted from a Baroque building called the Ermelerhaus, the Art'otel was designed by Johanna Nalbach in the 1990s. Choose between red, green, blue or aubergine rooms and contemplate the upside-down world of German painter George Baselitz on the walls. **Moderate**

Hotel Gendarm *old-world charm*

`5 D4`

Charlottenstrasse 61, Mitte • 030 20 60 66 0
>> www.hotel-gendarm-berlin.de

Sophisticated service, elegant rooms in Prussian blue and yellow, and a hearty breakfast buffet are among the features that make the 21-room Gendarm popular with business and leisure travellers alike. It is the perfect retreat close to bustling Friedrichstrasse, and the prices are unbeatable. **Moderate**

MitArt Hotel *art gallery-cum-pension*

`5 C1`

Linienstrasse 139–40, Mitte • 030 28 39 04 30
>> www.mitart.de

Owner Christiane Waszkowiak enthusiastically promotes the work of young artists in the breakfast room and bedrooms of this 19th-century boarding house. There are 30 guest rooms, all of which have private bathrooms. The district's cultural scene is just steps away. **Moderate**

Radisson SAS *rooms set around a fishbowl* `6 F2`

Karl-Liebknecht-Strasse 3, Mitte • 030 23 82 80
>> www.radissonsas.com

Located opposite the Fernsehturm (TV Tower) and historic Marienkirche, the Berlin branch of the Radisson SAS empire offers all the usual amenities of a top-class hotel, including a spa and business facilities. The unusual feature is the huge aquarium in its lobby. At 25 m (80 ft) high, this is purported to be the largest cylindrical aquarium in the world. It teems with 2,500 tropical fish. All guest rooms look either inward at the aquarium or outward across Berlin.

The rooms are cool, bright and airy, with Scandinavian-inspired decor. Health-conscious dining options include a noodle kitchen and the Mediterranean-Oriental fusion restaurant HEat [sic], which uses a tandoor oven and open grill. Order a coffee and sit and watch the fish in the Atrium Bar, or head for the more intimate Aqua Lounge for some sophisticated cocktails. **Expensive**

Berlin's Amazing Luxury Hotels

After the fall of the Wall in 1989, so many international hotel groups rushed into Berlin to build or acquire posh hotels that there is now an oversupply at the top end of the market. Visitors to Berlin enjoy some of the lowest rates for five-star hotels in Europe – as little as half the price for facilities and a level of service that might cost €400 or more in Paris, London or Milan. And even if some hotel groups have already given up and closed, others are still in the making.

Some of the new luxury hotels are an exercise in minimalism and modern art, as seen at the **Grand Hyatt** near Potsdamer Platz (Map 9 B1, Marlene-Dietrich-Pl. 2, 030 25 53 12 34, www.berlin.grand.hyatt.de), which was created by architect José Rafael Moneo and designer Hannes Wettstein. By contrast, the more traditional **Regent Berlin** (Map 5 D4, Charlottenstrasse 49, 030 20 33 66 66, www.theregentberlin.com) is fitted with 19th-century antiques and reproduction furniture, and has become a favourite with Hollywood stars.

Impeccable, friendly service is a trademark of the **Ritz-Carlton**, which opened in 2004 on Potsdamer Platz (Map 5 A5, 030 33 77 77, www.ritzcarlton.com). Financed by retail king Otto Beisheim, this hotel had a rough start (a fire and bad press) but appeals to visitors who appreciate huge furniture, thick carpets, heavy curtains and lashings of gold leaf. Equally opulent is Rocco Forte's **Hotel de Rome** (Map 5 A3, Behrenstrasse 37, 030 46 06 09 0, www.roccofortehotels.com), which opened in 2006 by the Brandenburger Tor.

Of the older luxury chain hotels, the **Westin Grand** (Map 5 C3, Friedrichstrasse 158–64, 030 20 27 0, www.westin-grand.com), set in a Socialist-era building, has been transformed into a very luxurious hotel with an impressive atrium lobby.

Artist Riverside *tiny art hotel* `5 C2`
Friedrichstrasse 106, Mitte • 030 28 49 00
>> www.great-hotel.com

This five-room art hotel caters to those who enjoy
eccentricity. The building's Soviet-style exterior belies
owner Uwe Buttgereit's flamboyant, vaguely 19th-
century style inside. Book the wedding suite if you'd
like to wallow in a freestanding bathtub with a view of
the Spree River. There's also a spa. **Moderate**

Honigmond *romantic hideaway* `3 C3`
Tieckstrasse 12, Mitte • 030 28 44 55 0
>> www.honigmond.de

The lovely Honigmond ("honeymoon"), occupying a
restored 19th-century mansion, is still one of Berlin's
best-kept secrets. Rooms are laid out with antiques;
some have four-poster beds. Further down the street,
the Honigmond Garden Hotel has guest rooms in the
mansion's former outbuildings. **Moderate**

InterContinental *first-class all round* `8 G1`
Budapester Strasse 2, Tiergarten • 030 26 02 0
>> www.interconti.com

The Interconti, as Berliners affectionately call this
popular hotel, is a city landmark – look out for the
modern, black-and-white chequered façade, fronted
by a pyramid of glass. The pyramid is part of the
lobby, which itself is the size of an airport check-in
hall and has been the setting for many grand balls.

   Despite tough competition from the new luxury
hotels in the east of the city, the Interconti is still one
of the most exclusive hotels in Berlin. Its success
owes much to a consistently professional and friendly
service that is often missing in other big hotels.
The spacious guest rooms have recently been
redesigned in subdued brown and beige hues.
Magnificent views across the city and the vast green
expanse of the Tiergarten are a big draw. Gourmet
restaurant Hugo's *(see p35)* and the intimate
Marlene bar are further attractions. **Expensive**

>> *Art hotels are among the exciting developments in Berlin's hotel scene*

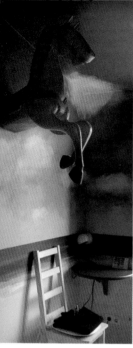

Künstlerheim Luise *creative rooms*

5 B2

Luisenstrasse 19, Mitte • 030 28 44 80
>> www.kuenstlerheim-luise.de

In one of the world's cultural capitals, it is not surprising to find some unusual hotels that have been created by artists and appeal to people with a liking for quirkiness. Foremost among these "art hotels" is the Künstlerheim Luise, which opened in 2001 and quickly became a hit with Germans and international visitors looking for that unique Berlin flair. Featuring contemporary works of art at every turn, the hotel has been described as "a gallery for sleeping over". The name of the hotel also hints at what is inside – Künstlerheim translates as "artists' asylum".

Each of the hotel's 50 rooms has been decorated by a contemporary artist. There are several ultra-minimalist, all-white, cell-like rooms. One room features a gigantic bed; in another, the bed hangs freely from the ceiling. A neon-lit installation is found in another room; a red horse jumps from the wall elsewhere. The artists are mainly Germans and include well-known painters such as Elvira Bach and Volker März. It's worth browsing the numbered rooms on the website to see the idiosyncratic vision of each artist. There are also works of art in the lobby, in the hallways and in a separate art gallery at the hotel. Information is readily available to explain the hotel's philosophy and the concept behind each artwork.

Part of the hotel is set in a restored Neo-Classical mansion dating from 1825: rooms here tend to be larger than in the wing built in 2003. However, rooms in the new wing have air-conditioning. Pricing partly depends on whether a room has a bathroom or not. Rooms in the Mansarde (an attic with sloping walls) are good budget options. The only drawback is the rather limited Continental breakfast. **Moderate**

Dorint Schweizerhof *sleek city hotel* `8 G1`
Budapester Strasse 25, Tiergarten • 030 26 96 0
>> www.dorint.com

Completely rebuilt in 1999, the Schweizerhof has
an appealingly modern aesthetic with its Bauhaus-
inspired colours and furnishings. Rooms are
surprisingly cosy and comfortable; the Superior
rooms have great views of the Tiergarten. It also has
one of the largest hotel pools in town. **Expensive**

The Mandala Hotel `5 A5`
Potsdamer Strasse 3, Tiergarten • 030 59 00 50 00 0
>> www.themandala.de

Relatively low-key among the high-rises on Potsdamer
Platz, this elegant apartment hotel is a five-star
establishment offering high-tech facilities. The suites
feature designer kitchenettes and working areas
suitable for business travellers. On the 5th floor is
the gourmet restaurant Facil *(see p34)*. **Expensive**

Bleibtreu *Mediterranean-inspired boutique hotel* `7 D2`
Bleibtreustrasse 31, Charlottenburg • 030 88 47 40
>> www.bleibtreu.com

Occupying a restored 19th-century building at the southern end of the
fashionable Bleibtreustrasse, the Bleibtreu is a tranquil retreat from
Charlottenburg's hectic streetlife. The hotel's airy rooms are individually
decorated, with an emphasis on soothing colours and natural fabrics.
There is a Mediterranean-style courtyard, a restaurant serving organic
dishes and an exceptionally good café, Deli 31 *(see p36)*. **Moderate**

Suites and Short-Stay Apartments
Berlin's growing significance as a political and
business centre has boosted the demand for
aparthotels. For businesspeople, good choices
include the **Mandala Suites Friedrichstrasse** (Map 5
C5, Friedrichstr. 185–90, 030 20 29 20, www.the
mandala.de), a four-star apartment hotel offering
kitchenettes and office facilities in all rooms

(see also The Mandala Hotel, above), and the
lower-priced **NH Berlin Heinrich-Heine** (Map 10 F1,
Heinrich Heine Platz 11, www.nh-hotels.com).
Budget options for long stays include the stylish
BHM Boardinghouse-Mitte (Map 4 E3, Mulackstr.
1–2, 030 28 04 53 06, www.boardinghouse-mitte.
com) and the **Econtel** (Map 1 C4, Soemmeringstr.
24, 030 34 68 10, www.econtel.de).

Savoy Hotel Berlin *classy city hotel* `8 F1`

Fasanenstrasse 9–10, Charlottenburg • 030 31 10 30
>> www.hotel-savoy.com

"A small hotel, but so pleasant and comfortable," wrote German Nobel laureate Thomas Mann (1875–1955) about Berlin's Savoy. His assessment still rings true, as this privately owned hotel, founded in 1929 and unconnected to the Savoys in London, Florence or Prague, holds its position above many newer hotels in the city. It stands on one of the most beautiful streets off Ku'damm and has long been favoured by a stylish, international clientele, including many writers, artists and actors (the Greta Garbo suite commemorates her visit). Rooms are elegant and spacious, and service is quietly attentive. The Times Bar is very British in style, with deep leather wing chairs. The Weinrot restaurant serves modern European cuisine and offers a particularly good deal for a two-course lunch. Also on the premises is one of Berlin's top cigar lounges, Casa del Habano. **Expensive**

Kempinski Bristol Berlin `8 F2`

Kurfürstendamm 27, Charlottenburg • 030 88 43 40
>> www.kempinskiberlin.de

Opened in 1952 by a surviving member of a prominent Jewish family, the "Kempi" began life as the lone star of West Berlin: a symbol of pompous, capitalist extravagance in the face of the grim Socialist regime on the other side of the Wall. Since then the hotel has adopted a more demure approach, and having undergone major renovations in the 1990s and a recent remodelling of its restaurant complex, it is one of the world's finest and most hospitable grand hotels.

Even by Berlin standards of affordability *(see p150)*, the hotel has some of the keenest-priced five-star rooms in town, tastefully adorned in blue, red and brown tones, and furnished with timeless, elegant furniture. You can expect a marble bathroom and all the usual little extras of a Kempinski hotel, as well as sound-proof windows. Set at the corner of Fasanenstrasse, it's well-placed for sightseeing. **Expensive**

Hotel Q! *lodgings for the 21st century* `8 E2`
Knesebeckstrasse 67, Charlottenburg • 030 81 00 66 0
>> www.hotel-q.de

A recent addition to Berlin's top hotels, Q! lives up to
its exclamation mark with a futuristic vision of urban
accommodation. From the outside it looks like a dull
office complex, and there is no name or sign on its
façade. Inside, however, is a series of amazing
roomscapes. Sloping walls and angled, illuminated
alcoves define spaces throughout, with monotone
reds, browns and whites predominating.

Nothing is accidental: a bed and a bath form a
continuous piece of furniture in one recess; another
alcove is just the right size for a flat-screen TV; and
red couches curve with the shape of your body. The
wellness area has a sand floor, and sound effects
take you to another world while you have a massage
or Japanese-style wash. The restaurant (Thai) and
bar are for guests or club members only: it's an
exclusive hotel – but not extortionate. **Moderate**

Ku'damm 101 *designer's dream hotel* `7 B3`
Kurfürstendamm 101, Wilmersdorf • 030 52 00 55 0
>> www.kudamm101.com

This ultra-modern, minimalist designer hotel is a far
cry from the flashy hotels of the early 1990s. Grey,
white and beige colours dominate; curvy furniture
and accessories complement the shiny surfaces.
The look will please those who like immaculate
design, but may seem a little austere to others.

Rooms are fairly spacious (partly because they are
so sparsely furnished). A real surprise are the New
York-style bathrooms – an intriguing mixture of
white retro tiles and state-of-the-art appliances.
Wireless LAN high-speed Internet access is standard
in all the rooms. With all this, it's no wonder that the
hotel quickly became a favourite of Germany's
media people and IT wizards. Equally progressive
are wellness services such as ear acupuncture and
the exotic Gua Sha pain relief therapy (it will change
the way you breathe). **Moderate**

AO Hostel Berlin Zoo *basic beds* 8 F1

Joachimsthaler Strasse 1–3, Charlottenburg
030 29 77 81 0
>> www.aobackpackers.de

It's set in an ugly building, but this hostel is popular with international backpackers looking simply for a clean bed in a central location. Dormitories have 8–10 beds; pay a bit more for a single or double room. There's a healthy breakfast buffet. **Cheap**

Brandenburger Hof *Bauhaus showroom* 8 F2

Eislebener Strasse 14, Charlottenburg • 030 21 40 50
>> www.brandenburger-hof.com

Parquet floors, stuccoed ceilings and a wealth of 1920s Bauhaus-style furniture and art define this classy, four-star establishment, which is set in a mansion on a quiet sidestreet near Ku'damm. Its Michelin-starred restaurant, Die Quadriga, has a lovely airy courtyard and atrium. **Expensive**

Propeller Island City Lodge 7 C3

Albrecht-Achilles-Strasse 58, Wilmersdorf
030 89 19 01 6
>> www.propeller-island.de

The owner claims the lodge is a true *Gesamtkunstwerk* ("work of art"), and it's certainly one of the most eccentric places to stay. Of the 45 individually designed rooms, one is decorated in a mood-altering vivid orange; the "griddle" room has nightmarish Surrealist imagery; and the "flying bed" room has a sloping floor. Only couples without inhibitions will appreciate the "mirror" room. Another is deliberately designed like a prison cell. Ask for the "clouds" room if you actually want to relax – it just has two huge photographs of clouds on either side of the bed.

The mastermind behind all this is Berlin artist Lars Stroschen, a jack-of-all-trades who has fulfilled a personal dream with this hotel. Service is limited: the breakfast room is modest, and some guests share bathrooms. But it's exciting for the price. **Cheap**

Booking Agencies

A simple way of booking a room is via the official **tourist board** (www.berlin-tourist-information.de or www.berlin.de, 030 25 00 25). The service is free and offers a best-price guarantee at many hotels. The **Hotel Reservation Service** (www.hrs.de, 0221 20 77 60 0) and **Avigo** (www.avigo.de, 0180 40 28 44 6) can access Berlin hotels in all price ranges.

A Berlin speciality is *Mitwohnzentralen* brokers, who arrange rooms in private homes. You can have an apartment to yourself or become part of a family or flat-sharing community. The top brokers are **Fine and Mine** (www.fineandmine.de, 030 23 55 12 0), **berlin-flats.com** (030 22 60 59 40) and **Mitwohnzentrale** (www.berlin-mitwohnzentrale.de, 030 61 82 00 8). Prices range from 25 to 100 euros a night.

Transit *an urban loft hotel*

Hagelberger Str. 53–4, Kreuzberg • 030 78 90 47 0
>> www.hotel-transit.com

A 19th-century, brick-built, industrial building in the heart of multicultural Kreuzberg has been transformed into a loft hotel with sparsely furnished, but bright and airy singles, doubles and dormitories. The breakfast buffet is the place to make friends with travellers from many other countries. **Cheap**

Relexa Schlosshotel Cecilienhof
Potsdam *historic apartments*

Neuer Garten, Potsdam • 033 13 70 50
>> www.relexa-hotel.de • Ⓢ Potsdam-Hauptbahnhof

The Cecilienhof palace was built in 1914–17 as the summer residence for the royal Hohenzollern family, and in 1945 it was the setting for the Potsdam Conference, which sealed Germany's fate after the war.

This is by far the most characterful and enticing hotel in Potsdam *(see pp142–3)*, and is well located for sightseeing and shopping in the town. The accommodation is modelled on a typical English country hotel, adorned with heavy draperies, polished furniture and antique lamps. The elegance of yesteryear is apparent, although some rooms are showing their age. Most rooms have an idyllic view of the Jungfernsee lake and park. You can tour the old royal apartments and historic conference room in which Truman, Stalin and Churchill signed the Allied Occupation policy. **Moderate**

Eastside Hotel *hotel by the Wall*

Mühlenstrasse 6, Friedrichshain • 030 29 38 34 00
>> www.eastsidecityhotel.de

This establishment makes up for its lack of amenities with a great (if traffic-ridden) location opposite the only substantial remaining section of the Wall. Rooms are small but very clean, and all have a bathroom. Singles have a view of the creatively decorated Wall. Prices include a modest breakfast buffet. **Cheap**

Almost every listing in this guide includes a page and grid reference to the maps in this section. The few entries that fall outside the area covered by these maps give transport details instead. The main map below shows the division of the Street Finder, along with the city's principal area names.

Greater Berlin

Key to Street Finder

🮔	Sight/public building	⊕	Hospital
⑤	S-Bahn station	⊜	Police station
⑪	U-Bahn station	✛	Church
✈	Airport	✡	Synagogue
🚉	Train station	⊗	Post Office
🚌	Coach station	▬	Pedestrian street
🚏	Main bus stop	⋯	Railway
Ⓟ	Parking	▬	Motorway

Scale of maps 1–4 and 7–11

0 metres · · · · · 600

0 yards · · · · · 600

Scale of maps 5–6

0 metres · · · · · 300

0 yards · · · · · 300

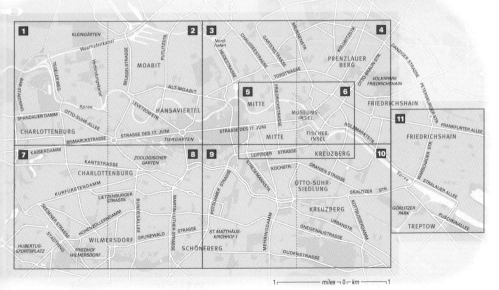

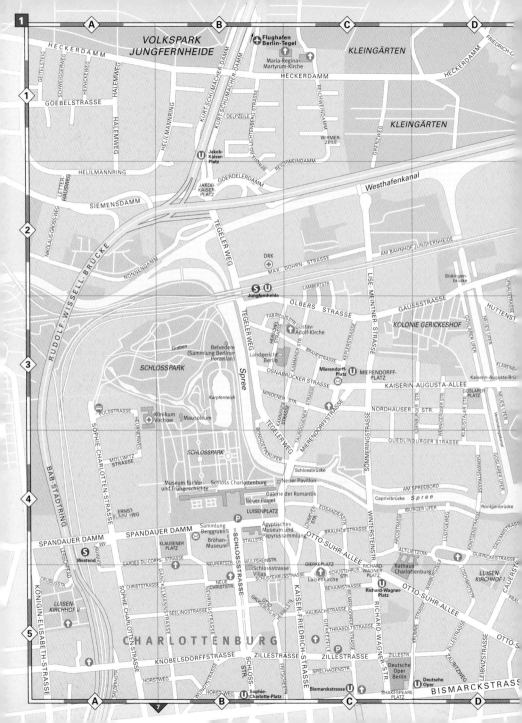

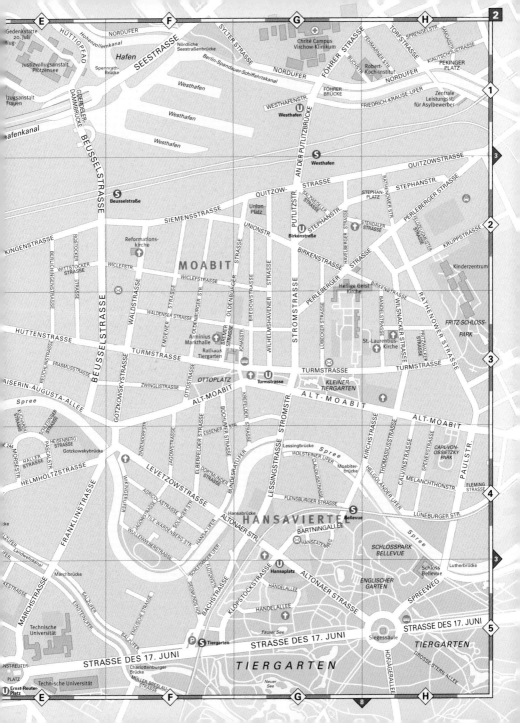

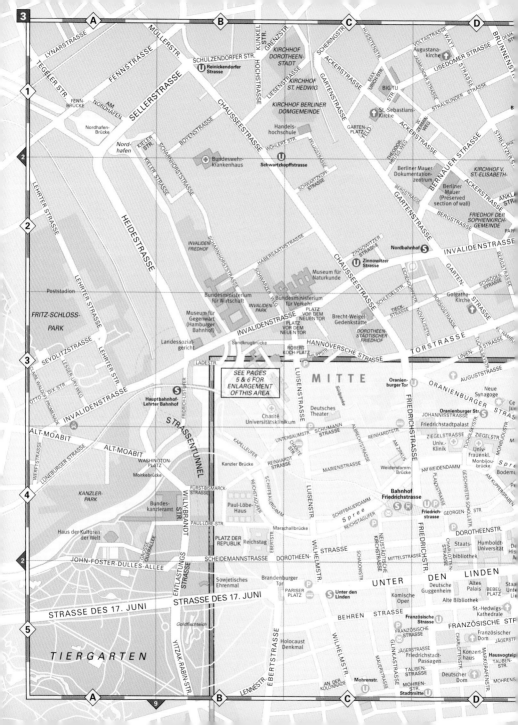

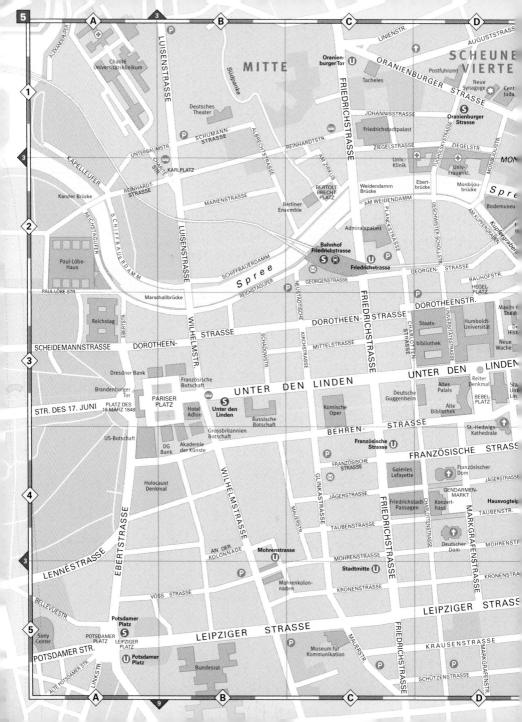

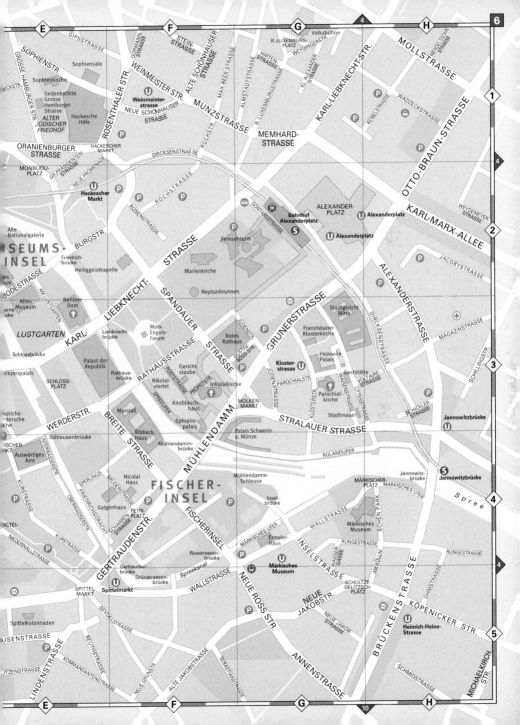

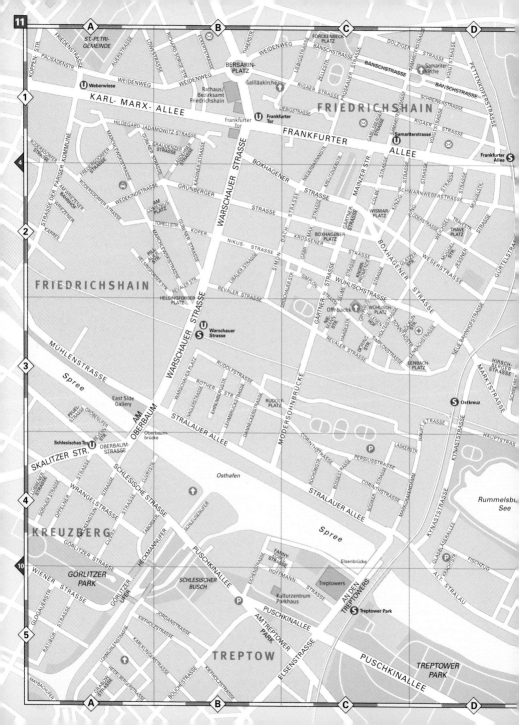

Index of Selected Streets

reference

Wherever you are in Berlin, whatever you are looking for, the pages that follow will direct you quickly to the relevant entries in the guide. As well as a general index, there are indexes that group entries by area and by type. For top tips on how to get to and around the city, and essential tourist information, see the transport and practical sections on pages 20–23.

Breathe (p58)
Cosmetics

Claudia Skoda Level (p54)
Fashion

Fiona Bennett (p51)
Hats

Fishbelly (p52)
Lingerie

Fluffy White Pink (p50)
Accessories

Friedrichstadtpassagen
(p126)
Shopping mall

Galeries Lafayette
(pp50 & 126)
Department store

Gendarmenmarkt
Christmas Market
(pp18–19)
Market

Hackesche Höfe (p125)
Shopping arcades

Hekticket (p91)
Tickets for shows

Hundt Hammer Stein (p53)
Books

Hut Up (p51)
Fashion

Interklassik (p91)
Tickets for shows

Kulturkaufhaus
Dussmann (p54)
CDs, videos and books

Lisa D. (p53)
Fashion

Made in Berlin (p52)
Vintage clothing

Neurotitan (p50)
Comics, records & CDs

RSVP (p53)
Stationery

Schön Einrichten (p52)
Furniture

Smart Travelling (p54)
Travel accessories

Sommerladen (p52)
Vintage clothing

Trippen (p52)
Shoes

Whisky & Cigars (p51)
Gourmet food and drink/cigars

Wunderkind Boutique (p53)
Fashion and bodycare products

Tiergarten

Arminius Markthalle (p62)
Market hall

Sony Center (p124)
Shopping mall

Strasse des 17. Juni
Markt (p62)
Antiques and art market

Art & Architecture

Charlottenburg

Bröhan Museum (p80)
Museum

Jewish Synagogue and
Community Centre (p128)
Religious building

Kaiser-Wilhelm-
Gedächtniskirche (p79)
Religious building

Löbbecke (p128)
Modern architecture

Museum Berggruen (p79)
Art collection

Museum für Fotographie (p79)
Art collection

Neues Kranzler Eck (p127)
Modern architecture

Olympiastadion (p81)
Historic sports stadium

Schloss Charlottenburg
(pp14, 69 & 80)
Palace

Mitte

Alte Nationalgalerie (p71)
Art collection

Ampelmann Galerie (p125)
Gallery and shop

Berliner Dom (p72)
Religious building

Brandenburger Tor
(pp13, 124 & 134)
Historic building

C/O (p73)
Contemporary art gallery

Deutsche Guggenheim (p73)
Contemporary art gallery

Deutsches Historisches
Museum (pp70 & 124)
Museum

Eigen + Art (p73)
Contemporary art gallery

Fernsehturm (pp68 & 72)
Modern architecture

Hackesche Höfe (p125)
Historic buildings

Holocaust Denkmal
(pp68 & 75)
Memorial

Kunst-Werke Berlin
(pp69 & 73)
Contemporary art gallery

Museumsinsel (p12)
Complex of museums

Neue Synagoge
(pp68 73 & 125)
Religious building and
museum

Pergamonmuseum (p70)
Museum

Sammlung Hoffman (p72)
Contemporary art gallery

Tacheles (p125)
Arts centre

Wohnmaschine (p73)
Contemporary art gallery

Tiergarten

Bauhaus-Archiv (p76)
Modern architecture and
museum

Filmmuseum Berlin (p76)
Museum

Gemäldegalerie (p78)
Art collection

Hamburger Bahnhof (p74)
Art collection

Haus der Kulturen
der Welt (p75)
Cultural complex

Kulturforum (p12)
Cultural complex

Kunstgewerbemuseum (p75)
Museum

Kupferstichkabinett (p76)
Art collection

Neue Nationalgalerie (p77)
Art collection

Reichstag (p13)
Historic building

Schloss Bellevue (p134)
Palace

Staatsbibliothek (p75)
Modern architecture

Performance

Charlottenburg

A-Trane (p93)
Jazz

Bamah Jüdisches
Theater (pp87 & 97)
Theatre

Literaturhaus Berlin (p128)
Literary venue

Quasimodo (pp86 & 92)
Jazz

Schaubühne (p94)
Theatre

Mitte

Berliner Ensemble,
Theater am
Schiffbauerdamm (pp87 & 88)
Theatre

Chamäleon (pp97 & 125)
Cabaret

Deutsches Theater
and DT Kammerspiele
(pp87 & 89)
Theatre

Distel (p97)
Cabaret

Honigmond (p151)
Moderate

Hotel de Rome (p150)
Expensive

Hotel Gendarm (p149)
Moderate

Künstlerheim Luise (p152)
Moderate

MitArt Hotel (p149)
Moderate

Radisson SAS (p150)
Expensive

Regent Berlin (p150)
Expensive

Westin Grand (p150)
Expensive

Tiergarten

Dorint Schweizerhof (p153)
Expensive

Grand Hyatt (p150)
Expensive

InterContinental (p151)
Expensive

Mandala Hotel (p153)
Moderate

Ritz-Carlton (p150)
Expensive

Wilmersdorf

**Propeller Island
City Lodge** (p156)
Cheap

South

Restaurants

Kreuzberg

Altes Zollhaus (p42) €€€
German

Café Adler (p116) €
Café

Café am Ufer
(pp30 & 129) €
Café

Defne (p42) €
Turkish

E.T.A. Hoffmann (p41) €€
French/German

Freischwimmer (p30) €
Café

Hasir (pp41 & 129) €
Turkish

Martin-Gropius-Bau Café
(pp83 & 129) €
Café

Sale e Tabacchi
(pp42 & 129) €€
Italian

Türkischer Markt
(pp62 & 129) €
Turkish

Schöneberg

Café M (p130) €
Café

KaDeWe Food Hall
(pp63 & 127) €
International

Mutter (p42) €€
International

Neuland Imbiss (p127) €
Currywurst

Shopping

Kreuzberg

Dawn (p52)
Vintage clothing

**Die Imaginäre Manufaktur/
DIM** (p64)
Homewares

Grober Unfug (p64)
Comics

**Kottbusser Tor
Markt** (p129)
Fruit market

Marheinecke Markthalle
(p62)
Market hall

Space Hall (p54)
CDs and records

Türkischer Markt (p62)
Middle Eastern market

Schöneberg

KaDeWe (pp63 & 127)
Department store

Winterfeldplatz Markt (p130)
Market

Wittenbergplatz Markt
(p63)
Food market

Art & Architecture

Kreuzberg

Anhalter Bahnhof (p129)
Historic building

Berlinische Galerie (p73)
Contemporary art gallery

Berlin Wall Remains (p130)
Historic site

Checkpoint Charlie
(pp14 & 129)
Historic site

**Deutsches
Technikmuseum** (p81)
Museum

Jüdisches Museum (p82)
*Museum and modern
architecture*

Martin-Gropius-Bau
(pp83 & 129)
Exhibition space

**Topographie des
Terrors** (p81)
Museum

Performance

Kreuzberg

Babylon (p95)
Cinema

BKA Kreuzberg (p89)
Avant-garde music

Eiszeit (p95)
Cinema

Galerie Tristesse (p128)
Performing arts

Hebbel am Ufer/HAU (p93)
*Performing arts/
mixed venue*

Tempodrom (p129)
Music venue

Yorckschlösschen (p95)
Jazz

Schöneberg

Bar Jeder Vernunft (p97)
Cabaret

Odeon (p95)
Cinema

Bars & Clubs

Kreuzberg

Ankerklause (p111)
Bar

Arcanoa (p106)
Lounge bar

Bierhimmel (p111)
Lounge bar & café

Haifischbar (p114)
Cocktail bar

Heinz Minki (p128)
Bar

Kaiserstein (p116)
Beer garden

Konrad Tönz (p114)
DJ bar

Madonna (p111)
Bar

Orient Lounge (p106)
Lounge bar

Rote Rosen (p110)
Bar & venue

Verein der Visionäre
(p106)
Lounge bar

Watergate
(pp111 & 128)
Dance club & lounge bar

Wirtschaftwunder (p114)
Cocktail bar

Würgeengel (p135)
Cocktail bar

Magazin (p96)
Contemporary art gallery

Sowjetisches Ehrenmahl
(p136)
Memorial

Performance

Friedrichshain

Maria am Ufer (pp86 & 95)
Music venue

Tempelhof
Columbiahalle/club (p95)
Live rock and pop

Treptow
Arena Treptow (pp86 & 96)
Live rock and pop

Glashaus (p96)
Theatre

Bars & Clubs

Friedrichshain

Black Girls Coalition (p117)
Club

Goldfisch (p130)
Bar

Himmelreich (p130)
Bar

K17 (p117)
Dance club

Matrix (p118)
Dance club

Narva Lounge (p119)
Club

**Panorama Bar/
Berghain** (p117)
Dance club

YAAM (p118)
Beach bar & club

Treptow

MS Hoppetosse
(p117)
Riverboat bar & club

Streetlife

Friedrichshain (p130)
District

Havens

Treptow

Arena Badeschiff (p137)
Bathing ship

Treptower Park (p136)
Park

Hotels

Friedrichshain

Eastside Hotel (p157)
Cheap

North

Restaurants

Prenzlauer Berg

Drei (pp45 & 131)   €€
International

Frannz (p45)   €€
German

Gugelhof
(pp44 & 131)   €€
French/Swiss

Khushi (p45)   €
Indian

Pasternak (pp45 & 131)   €€
Russian

Zander (p131)   €€
European

Shopping

Prenzlauer Berg

Luxus International (p65)
Accessories

Ökomarkt (p131)
Market

Vopo Records (p54)
CDs and records

Art & Architecture

Prenzlauer Berg

Kulturbrauerei (p131)
*Historic buildings and
cultural complex*

Wasserturm (p131)
Historic building

Weissensee

Mies van der Rohe
Haus (p83)
*Modern architecture and
exhibition space*

Performance

Prenzlauer Berg

Bastard
(pp96 & 131)
Literary venue

Knaack Club (p96)
Live music venue

Kulturbrauerei (p131)
Mixed venues

Magnet Club (p97)
Live music venue

Bars & Clubs

Prenzlauer Berg

Frannz Club (p121)
Dance club

Gagarin (p119)
Bar

Icon (p120)
Dance club

Kulturbrauerei (p131)
Mixed venues

NBI (p120)
Lounge bar

Prater
(pp116 & 131)
Beer garden

Restauration 1900
(p131)
Bar

Schwarzsauer (p119)
Cocktail bar

Scotch & Sofa (p106)
Lounge bar

Seven Lounge (p106)
Lounge bar

X-Bar (p106)
Lounge bar

Streetlife

Prenzlauer Berg (p131)
District

Restaurants

Asian

Pan Asia (p31) €€
Centre/Mitte

Austrian

Lutter & Wegner (p29) €€
Centre/Mitte

Bakeries

Bagel Station (p30) €
Centre/Mitte

Cafés & Coffee Houses

Adlon Café (p124) €
Centre/Mitte

Barcomi's Deli (p30) €
Centre/Mitte

Beth Café (p125) €
Centre/Mitte

Café Adler (p116) €
South/Kreuzberg

Café am Engelbecken €
(p136)
Centre/Mitte

Café am Neuen See €
(pp116 & 134)
Centre/Tiergarten

Café am Ufer (pp30 & 129) €
South/Kreuzberg

Café Balzac (p127) €
Centre/Charlottenburg

Café Carras (p127) €
Centre/Charlottenburg

Café Einstein €
(pp30, 124 & 135)
Centre/Mitte & Tiergarten

Café M (p130) €
South/Schöneberg

Café Möhring (p126) €
Centre/Mitte

Café Orange (pp33 & 125) €
Centre/Mitte

Café Savigny €
(pp30 & 126)
Centre/Charlottenburg

Deli 31 (p36) €
Centre/Charlottenburg

Freischwimmer (p30) €
South/Kreuzberg

Grunewaldturm (p141) €
Southwest/Grunewald

Konditorei Buchwald (p134) €
Centre/Tiergarten

Lindenlife (p124) €
Centre/Mitte

Martin-Gropius-Bau €
Café (pp83 & 129)
South/Kreuzberg

Opernpalais (pp30 & 124) €€
Centre/Mitte

Tacheles Café (p125) €
Centre/Mitte

Wintergarten Café (p128) €
Centre/Charlottenburg

Currywurst

Neuland Imbiss (p127) €
South/Schöneberg

European

Ali Baba (p36) €
Centre/Charlottenburg

Weinhaus Huth (p124) €€
Centre/Tiergarten

Zander (p131) €€
North/Prenzlauer Berg

French

Borchardt (p28) €€€
Centre/Mitte

E.T.A. Hoffmann (p41) €€
South/Kreuzberg

Gugelhof (pp44 & 131) €€
North/Prenzlauer Berg

Juliette (p44) €€€
Southwest/Potsdam

Fusion

Oktogon Fusion (p33) €€€
Centre/Tiergarten

Zoe (p33) €€
Centre/Mitte

German

Altes Zollhaus (p42) €€€
South/Kreuzberg

Die Fischerhütte (p140) €
Southwest/Schlachtensee

Diekmann im €€€
Châlet Suisse (p43)
Southwest/Grunewald

Engelbecken (p40) €
Centre/Charlottenburg

E.T.A. Hoffmann (p41) €€
South/Kreuzberg

Florian (p40) €€
Centre/Charlottenburg

Forsthaus Paulsborn €€
(p43)
Southwest/Grunewald

Frannz (p45) €€
North/Prenzlauer Berg

Hackescher Hof (p31) €€
Centre/Mitte

Haus Berlin (pp44 & 130) €€
East/Friedrichshain

Hugo's (p35) €€€
Centre/Tiergarten

Remise im Schloss €€€
Klein-Glienicke (p43)
Southwest/Wannsee

Schloss Cecilienhof €€€
(p143)
Southwest/Potsdam

Vau (p30) €€€
Centre/Mitte

Zur Letzten Instanz (p33) €
Centre/Mitte

Indian

Khushi (p45) €
North/Prenzlauer Berg

International

Drei (pp45 & 131) €€
North/Prenzlauer Berg

Facil (p34) €€€
Centre/Tiergarten

German

KaDeWe Food Hall €
(pp63 & 127)
South/Schöneberg

Lubitsch (p126) €€
Centre/Charlottenburg

Margaux (p30) €€€
Centre/Mitte

MS Hoppetosse (p117) €€
East/Treptow

Mutter (p42) €€
South/Schöneberg

Speckers zur €€
Ratswaage (p143)
Southwest/Potsdam

Vox (p35) €€€
Centre/Tiergarten

Italian

Bocca di Bacco (p29) €€€
Centre/Mitte

Brunello (p126) €€
Centre/Charlottenburg

Noiquattro €€
(pp44 & 130)
East/Friedrichshain

Sale e Tabacchi €€
(pp42 & 129)
South/Kreuzberg

Schwarzenraben (p32) €€€
Centre/Mitte

Via Condotti (p128) €€
Centre/Charlottenburg

Japanese

Kuchi (p37) €€
Centre/Charlottenburg

Mediterranean

Villa Kellermann (p143) €€
Southwest/Potsdam

Pizza

Ali Baba (p36) €
Centre/Charlottenburg

XII Apostel (p36) €€
Centre/Charlottenburg

Russian

Blockhaus Nikolskoe €€
(p140)
Southwest/Wannsee

Pasternak (pp45 & 131) €€
North/Prenzlauer Berg

Spanish

Mar y Sol (p40) €€
Centre/Charlottenburg

Swiss

Diekmann im €€€
Châlet Suisse (p43)
Southwest/Grunewald

Gugelhof €€
(pp44 & 131)
North/Prenzlauer Berg

Turkish

Defne (p42) €
South/Kreuzberg

Hasir (pp40 & 129) €
South/Kreuzberg

Türkischer Markt €
(pp62 & 129)
South/Kreuzberg

Vietnamese

Monsieur Vuong (p32) €
Centre/Mitte

Shopping

Accessories

Andreas Murkudis (p55)
Centre/Mitte

Fluffy White Pink (p50)
Centre/Mitte

Luxus International (p65)
North/Prenzlauer Berg

Porsche Design Store (p59)
Centre/Charlottenburg

Röckl Handschuhe (p128)
Centre/Charlottenburg

Art and Antiques

Gipsformerei (p59)
Centre/Charlottenburg

Kunst und Nostalgie
Markt (p124)
Centre/Mitte

Strasse des 17. Juni
Markt (p62)
Centre/Tiergarten

Villa Grisebach (p128)
Centre/Charlottenburg

Bodycare Products

Wunderkind Boutique (p53)
Centre/Mitte

Books

Berlin-Story (pp49 & 124)
Centre/Mitte

Bücherbogen (pp60 & 126)
Centre/Charlottenburg

Hugendubel (p62)
Centre/Charlottenburg

Hundt Hammer Stein (p53)
Centre/Mitte

Kohlhaas & Company (p128)
Centre/Charlottenburg

Kulturkaufhaus
Dussmann (p54)
Centre/Mitte

Cigars

Whisky & Cigars (p51)
Centre/Mitte

Comics

Grober Unfug (p64)
South/Kreuzberg

Neurotitan (p50)
Centre/Mitte

Cosmetics

Breathe (p58)
Centre/Mitte

Manufactum (p59)
Centre/Charlottenburg

Department Stores

Galeries Lafayette
(pp50 & 126)
Centre/Mitte

KaDeWe (pp63 & 127)
South/Schöneberg

Peek & Cloppenburg (p127)
Centre/Charlottenburg

Fashion

Andreas Murkudis (p55)
Centre/Mitte

Apartment (p58)
Centre/Mitte

Belleville (p58)
Centre/Mitte

Berlinomat (p65)
East/Friedrichshain

Claudia Skoda Level (p54)
Centre/Mitte

Hut Up (p51)
Centre/Mitte

Jil Sander (p58)
Centre/Charlottenburg

Lisa D. (p53)
Centre/Mitte

Patrick Hellmann (p60)
Centre/Charlottenburg

Wunderkind Boutique (p53)
Centre/Mitte

Furniture

Dopo Domani (p61)
Centre/Charlottenburg

Schön Einrichten (p52)
Centre/Mitte

Stilwerk (p60)
Centre/Charlottenburg

Gourmet Food and Drink

Brot & Butter (p59)
Centre/Charlottenburg

Butter-Lindner (p60)
Centre/Charlottenburg

KaDeWe Sixth Floor
(pp63 & 127)
South/Schöneberg

Karl-August-Platz
Markt (p62)
Centre/Charlottenburg

Melanie (p62)
Centre/Charlottenburg

Ökomarkt (p131)
North/Prenzlauer Berg

Türkischer Markt (p62)
South/Kreuzberg

Whisky & Cigars (p51)
Centre/Mitte

Winterfeldplatz Markt (p130)
South/Schöneberg

Wittenbergplatz Markt (p62)
South/Schöneberg

Hats

Fiona Bennett (p51)
Centre/Mitte

Homewares

Andreas Murkudis (p55)
Centre/Mitte

Die Imaginäre Manufaktur/
DIM (p64)
South/Kreuzberg

Dopo Domani (p61)
Centre/Charlottenburg

Manufactum (p59)
Centre/Charlottenburg

Schön Einrichten (p52)
Centre/Mitte

Stilwerk (p60)
Centre/Charlottenburg

Lingerie

Blush (p58)
Centre/Mitte

Fishbelly (p52)
Centre/Mitte

Markets

Arminius Markthalle (p62)
Centre/Tiergarten

Index by Type

Performance

Literary Venues

Bastard (pp96 & 131)
North/Prenzlauer Berg

Literaturhaus Berlin (p128)
Centre/Charlottenburg

Live Rock and Pop Music

Arena Treptow (p96)
East/Treptow

Bastard (pp96 & 131)
North/Prenzlauer Berg

Columbiahalle/club (p95)
East/Tempelhof

Knaack Club (p96)
North/Prenzlauer Berg

Magnet Club (p97)
North/Prenzlauer Berg

Mixed Venues

Arena Treptow (p96)
East/Treptow

Haus der Kulturen der Welt (p93)
Centre/Tiergarten

Hebbel am Ufer/HAU (p93)
South/Kreuzberg

Kulturbrauerei (p131)
North/Prenzlauer Berg

Kulturforum (p12)
Centre/Tiergarten

Sony Center (p124)
Centre/Tiergarten

Tempodrom (p129)
South/Kreuzberg

Volksbühne (p90)
Centre/Mitte

Performing Arts

Galerie Tristesse (p128)
South/Kreuzberg

Haus der Kulturen der Welt (p93)
Centre/Tiergarten

Hebbel am Ufer/HAU (p93)
South/Kreuzberg

Sophiensäle (p90)
Centre/Mitte

Volksbühne (p90)
Centre/Mitte

Theatres

Bamah Jüdisches Theater (p97)
Centre/Charlottenburg

Berliner Ensemble, Theater am Schiffbauerdamm (p88)
Centre/Mitte

Deutsches Theater and DT Kammerspiele (p89)
Centre/Mitte

Glashaus (p96)
East/Treptow

Hebbel am Ufer/HAU (p93)
South/Kreuzberg

Schaubühne (p94)
Centre/Charlottenburg

Theater am Potsdamer Platz (p92)
Centre/Tiergarten

Volksbühne (p90)
Centre/Mitte

Bars & Clubs

Beach Bars

Bundespressestrand (p116)
Centre/Tiergarten

Strandbar (p116)
Centre/Mitte

YAAM (p118)
East/Friedrichshain

Beer Gardens

Die Fischerhütte (p142)
Southwest/Schlachtensee

Kaiserstein (p116)
South/Kreuzberg

Kastanie (p116)
Centre/Charlottenburg

Loretta am Wannsee (p116)
Southwest/Wannsee

Prater (pp116 & 131)
North/Prenzlauer Berg

Cocktail/Lounge Bars

Ambulance Bar (p107)
Centre/Mitte

Arcanoa (p106)
South/Kreuzberg

Bar am Lützowplatz (p108)
Centre/Tiergarten

Bierhimmel (p111)
South/Kreuzberg

Billy Wilder's (p124)
Centre/Tiergarten

Café Moskau (p103)
Centre/Mitte

Erdbeerbar (p106)
Centre/Mitte

Green Door (pp116 & 130)
South/Schöneberg

Haifischbar (p114)
South/Kreuzberg

Josty Bar (pp106 & 124)
Centre/Tiergarten

Lumumba (p104)
Centre/Mitte

NBI (p120)
North/Prenzlauer Berg

Newton Bar (p106)
Centre/Mitte

Orient Lounge (p106)
South/Kreuzberg

Paris Bar / Le Bar du Paris Bar (p109)
Centre/Charlottenburg

Schwarzsauer (p119)
North/Prenzlauer Berg

Scotch & Sofa (p106)
North/Prenzlauer Berg

Seven Lounge (p106)
North/Prenzlauer Berg

Verein der Visionäre (p106)
South/Kreuzberg

Victoria Bar (p109)
Centre/Tiergarten

Wirtschaftwunder (p114)
South/Kreuzberg

Würgeengel (p135)
South/Kreuzberg

X-Bar (p106)
North/Prenzlauer Berg

Dance Clubs

Abraxas (p110)
Centre/Charlottenburg

Berghain (p117)
East/Friedrichshain

Big Eden (p110)
Centre/Charlottenburg

Bohannon (p102)
Centre/Mitte

Frannz Club (p121)
North/Prenzlauer Berg

Havanna (p116)
South/Schöneberg

Icon (p120)
North/Prenzlauer Berg

K17 (p117)
East/Friedrichshain

Kaffee Burger (p105)
Centre/Mitte

Matrix (p118)
East/Friedrichshain

Mudd Club (p107)
Centre/Mitte

Narva Lounge (p119)
East/Friedrichshain

Panorama Bar/ Berghain (p117)
East/Friedrichshain

Rio (p106)
Centre/Mitte

Sage Club (p103)
Centre/Mitte

Trompete (p109)
Centre/Tiergarten

Watergate
(pp111 & 128)
South/Kreuzberg

Pubs and DJ Bars

Ankerklause (p111)
South/Kreuzberg

Club der Polnischen
Versager (p105)
Centre/Mitte

Felix (p108)
Centre/Mitte

Gagarin (p119)
North/Prenzlauer Berg

Goldfisch (p130)
East/Friedrichshain

Heinz Minki (p128)
South/Kreuzberg

Himmelreich (p130)
East/Friedrichshain

King Kong Klub (p105)
Centre/Mitte

Kilkenny Irish Pub (p107)
Centre/Mitte

KMA 36 (p103)
Centre/Mitte

Konrad Tönz (p114)
South/Kreuzberg

Madonna (p111)
South/Kreuzberg

MS Hoppetosse (p117)
East/Treptow

Restauration 1900
(p131)
North/Prenzlauer Berg

Rote Rosen (p110)
South/Kreuzberg

Sharon Stonewall
(p108)
Centre/Mitte

Slumberland (p130)
South/Schöneberg

Sophienclub (p108)
Centre/Mitte

Sternradio (p103)
Centre/Mitte

Tacheles (p125)
Centre/Mitte

Z-Bar (p106)
Centre/Mitte

Sex/Gender Theme Clubs

Black Girls Coalition
(p117)
East/Friedrichshain

KitKat Club (p115)
South/Schöneberg

Havens

Cafés and Bars

Café am Engelbecken
(p136)
Centre/Mitte

Café Einstein (p135)
Centre/Tiergarten

Würgeengel (p135)
South/Kreuzberg

Nature Reserves and Lakes

Grunewald Forest (p141)
Southwest/Grunewald

Heiliger See (p142)
Southwest/Potsdam

Schlachtensee (p140)
Southwest/Schlahtensee

Taufelsee (p141)
Southwest/Grunewald

Parks and Gardens

Botanischer Garten (p137)
South/Dahlem

Klein-Glienicke (p140)
Southwest/Wannsee

Luisenstädtischer Kanal
(p136)
South/Kreuzberg

Park Sanssouci (p142)
Southwest/Potsdam

Pfaueninsel (p140)
Southwest/Wannsee

Neuer Garten (p142)
Southwest/Potsdam

Tiergarten (p134)
Centre/Tiergarten

Treptower Park (p136)
East/Treptow

Spas and Swimming

Arena Badeschiff (p137)
East/Treptow

Die Banja (p137)
South/Dahlem

Sultan Hamam (p136)
South/Schöneberg

Thermen am
Europa-Center (p135)
Centre/Tiergarten

Hotels

Cheap

AO Hostel Berlin Zoo
(p156)
Centre/Charlottenburg

Eastside Hotel (p157)
East/Friedrichshain

Propeller Island
City Lodge (p156)
Centre/Wilmersdorf

Transit (p157)
South/Kreuzberg

Moderate

Artist Riverside (p151)
Centre/Mitte

Art'otel Berlin Mitte
(p149)
Centre/Mitte

Bleibtreu (p153)
Centre/Charlottenburg

Honigmond (p151)
Centre/Mitte

Hotel Gendarm (p149)
Centre/Mitte

Hotel Q! (p155)
Centre/Charlottenburg

Ku'damm 101 (p155)
Centre/Charlottenburg

Künstlerheim Luise
(p152)
Centre/Mitte

Mandala Hotel (p153)
Centre/Tiergarten

MitArt Hotel (p149)
Centre/Mitte

Relexa Schlosshotel
Cecilienhof Potsdam
(p157)
Southwest/Potsdam

Expensive

Adlon Kempinski (p148)
Centre/Mitte

Brandenburger Hof
(p156)
Centre/Charlottenburg

Dorint Schweizerhof
(p153)
Centre/Tiergarten

Dorint-Sofitel am
Gendarmenmarkt
(p149)
Centre/Mitte

Grand Hyatt (p150)
Centre/Tiergarten

Hotel de Rome (p150)
Centre/Mitte

InterContinental (p151)
Centre/Mitte

Kempinski Bristol Berlin
(p154)
Centre/Charlottenburg

Radisson SAS (p150)
Centre/Mitte

Regent Berlin (p150)
Centre/Mitte

Ritz-Carlton (p150)
Centre/Tiergarten

Savoy Hotel Berlin (p154)
Centre/Charlottenburg

Westin Grand (p150)
Centre/Mitte

General Index

General Index

Acknowledgments

Produced by Blue Island Publishing
www.blueisland.co.uk
Editorial Director Rosalyn Thiro
Art Director Stephen Bere
Commissioning Editor Michael Ellis
Fact Checker Constance Hanna
Proofreader Stewart Wild
Picture Researcher Brigitte Arora

Published by DK
Publishing Managers Jane Ewart and Scarlett O'Hara
Senior Editor Christine Stroyan
Senior Designers Paul Jackson and Marisa Renzullo
Website Editor Gouri Banerji
Cartographic Editor Casper Morris
Senior Cartographer Uma Bhattacharya
DTP Designers Jason Little and Natasha Lu
Production Coordinator Linda Dare
Fact Checker Jürgen Scheunemann

PHOTOGRAPHY PERMISSIONS

The publishers would like to thank all the restaurants, shops, bars, clubs, museums and other establishments for their assistance and kind permission to photograph their premises.

Placement Key: tc = top centre; tl = top left; tr = top right; br = bottom right; bl = bottom left; blc = bottom left centre; c = centre; cl = centre left; cr = centre right

The publishers would like to thank the following companies and picture libraries for permission to reproduce their photographs:

ALAMY IMAGES: travelstock44.de l.

BERLIN TOURISMUS MARKETING GMBH: 90 blc.

CORBIS: CNP/Ron Sachs 14cl, 15tr; Paul Hardy 11tc; Jon Hicks 13br; Reuters/Christian Charisius 17tl; Zefa/Svenja-Foto 13cr.

DELI 31 BLEIBTREU: 36bl.

GETTY IMAGES: Taxi/Gerd Schnuerer 6–7.

MUSEUM FÜR FOTOGRAFIE: 79cl.

NEUE NATIONALGALERIE: Henry Moore Foundation 77bl.
NEUROTITA: Henryk Weiffenbach 50bl.

SAVOY HOTEL BERLIN: 154tl/tr.
GUENTER SCHNEIDER: 140tl.
STASI MUSEUM: 83cl.

Full Page Picture Captions
Fernsehturm (TV Tower): 2; Watergate: 8–9; Vox: 24–5; Schwarzenraben: 38–9; Stilwerk: 46–7; Budapester Schuhe: 56–7; Holocaust Denkmal: 66–7; A-Trane: 84–5; Sage Club: 98–9; Felix: 112–13; Friedrichshain (East Side Gallery): 122–3; Park Sanssouci, Potsdam: 132–3; Arena Badeschiff: 138–9; Ku'damm 101: 144–5; Potsdamer Platz: 158.

Jacket Images
Front: ALAMY IMAGES: travelstock44.de.
Back: DK images: all.

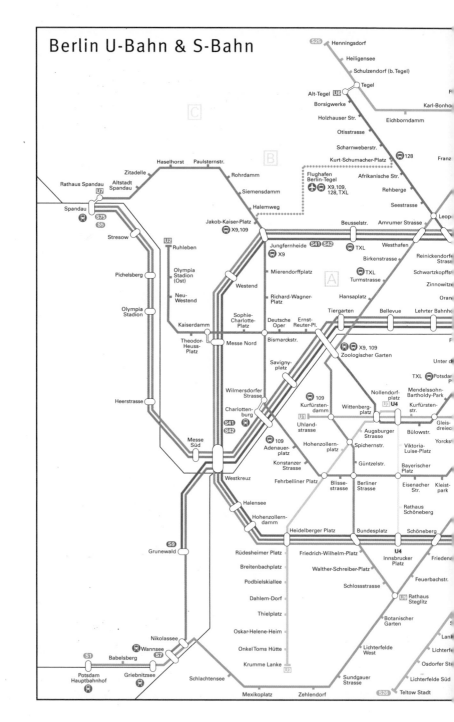

Berlin U-Bahn & S-Bahn